WOODCARVING
SIMPLIFIED

WOODCARVING SIMPLIFIED

Graciela L. Fazzalare

CHILTON BOOK COMPANY

RADNOR, PENNSYLVANIA

Copyright © 1983 by Graciela L. Fazzalare
All Rights Reserved
Published in Radnor, Pennsylvania 19089,
by Chilton Book Company
Designed by William E. Lickfield
Manufactured in the United States of America

Library of Congress Cataloging in Publication Data
Fazzalare, Graciela L.
    Woodcarving simplified.
    Includes index.
    1. Wood-carving.   I. Title.
TT199.7.F38   1983   731.4′62   83-70780
ISBN 0-8019-7148-9
ISBN 0-8019-7149-7 (pbk.)

1 2 3 4 5 6 7 8 9 0   2 1 0 9 8 7 6 5 4 3

Contents

Chapter 3
Tool Grips, Wood Cuts and Techniques   53

Acknowledgments

MANY artists and friends were of immeasurable help in putting this book together, but several people deserve special gratitude: To my parents, who gave me support along the way; to Richard Sniffin for his photographs, and to Richard Carafelli for his advice and help with the photography; to Clark Mester for allowing me into his studio, and for his friendship; to Ben Porter, for allowing me to photograph his lovely pieces, and to Mrs. Porter for her kindness and patience; and most of all to Vincent Fazzalare for his assistance, understanding, and love.

WOODCARVING SIMPLIFIED

Introduction

WOODCARVING has existed among different cultures for centuries—from primitive African wood sculpture to colonial American folk art. Early in this century, however, artists and sculptors such as Picasso, Constantin Brancusi, Jean Arp, Henry Moore, and Barbara Hepworth began to explore organic, natural forms using wood as the medium, influenced in part by African tribal masks and primitive sculpture.

Picasso carried these forms over into painting, then sculpture, in his Cubist period, as did Jean Arp, one of the founders of Dadaism. Brancusi was another sculptor who turned away from traditional representational sculpture, and he refined his highly polished, curvilinear pieces even further to produce a harmonious fusion of form and medium.

But it was perhaps Henry Moore and his fondness for direct carving, combined with his abstract, organic vocabulary in his early reclining figures, who made wood a respectable medium in modern art. And in the footsteps of Moore, British sculptor Barbara Hepworth became one of the first major artists to use wood as an integral statement in her geometric constructions and organic figures.

Today, wood sculptures, both representational and abstract, stand proudly alongside the bronzes and marbles in every major museum of the world.

For the beginning woodcarver, imagination, inspiration, a few good tools, and some pieces of wood are all that are necessary for woodcarving and whittling. Many texts have been published to educate the novice on the ways of wood, but I hope to go one step further—or rather, a step less—and *guide* the novice. For the student of woodcarving and whittling, there are better technical manuals, but this book is for doing, and for learning by doing. Its purpose is to encourage, support, inspire, and guide.

Nothing is absolute with wood. Anyone with the desire can carve and whittle. If you feel that you cannot do delicate details, try carving shapes. If you feel that your shapes are not accurate or precise, try doing abstract forms. The point is to learn and practice—then create. There are no set ways to carve or whittle. With tools in hand, you become the creator and the experimenter—the *artist*.

CHAPTER 1

Characteristics and Types of Wood

WOODCARVING encompasses many tools, techniques, and finished products. In particular, it employs chisels and gouges for the express purpose of removing extraneous wood from a block to create a specific form. Or as my grandfather put it, "If you want to make a dog, just knock off all the parts that don't look like a dog."

At one end of the spectrum in woodcarving is sculpture and at the other end is relief, or two-dimensional, carving. With practice and experimentation, you will begin to discover your individual preferences, and soon you will develop a personal style. There are so many tools and types of wood that, with a basic background in both, the novice woodcarver will soon develop individual preferences.

This chapter will include the woods traditionally used in woodcarving and whittling. These are the most well-known, readily available, tried-and-true woods. Some types of wood that, for one reason or another, are not well suited for carving and whittling are listed so that you will know which ones to avoid.

In woodcarving, it matters little which comes first—

the design or the piece of wood. Whichever one you start with will usually inspire the other. If the emphasis of the design is on shape and form rather than on detail, the best types of woods would be those with characteristics that lend themselves to being the main attraction. A flashy piece of cedar, for instance, might need little embellishment because the grain and color themselves are eyecatching. On the other hand, a tight-grained white pine has no distinguishable grain to detract from the carved or whittled details. It all comes down to personal preference mixed with some common sense about how to enhance each piece of wood according to its individual characteristics. Luckily, nature provides a wide variety of grains and textures within each species of wood to allow individual choice and unique appearance.

Before you choose a type of wood, decide whether you want to whittle it or carve it with tools. Try to visualize the finished piece with all its details. As you work the wood, stop from time to time and look at it from all angles. Notice the grain, the color variations, and any unusual burrs or markings. Even cracks in the wood can be used to good advantage. At any point, you may leave it rough, add more detail, or polish it to a high gloss. Each piece is as individual as the tree it came from. By incorporating design with color, grain, and texture and blending them harmoniously, even as a beginner, you will find woodcarving a rewarding craft.

Nature is neither consistent nor predictable. Wood and its characteristics vary from tree to tree even within the same species. Within certain limitations, however, woods can be labeled and grouped according to attributes common to each species.

Fig. 1-1 *"Nativity Scene," by Dick Salazar. This beautifully detailed, carved set has a painted finish.*

Grain (growth and figure patterns), color, and hardness and softness of the wood are the three main methods of grouping. Before you choose the type of wood for a specific project, consider each of these three basics.

Understanding how a tree grows and how its wood is formed may help in understanding why certain attributes are desirable for certain designs. Wood is composed of slender vertical "tubes" that function

Fig. 1-2 *This unusual piece by Dick Salazar was carved from an unfinished log. The features are rustic, and blend with the rough wood exterior.*

as support for the tree. The young, softer, sap-bearing wood is called *sapwood.* These tubular fibers are perpendicularly crossed by other, horizontal fibers that also transport nourishment, and these fibers compose the wood rays.

In addition to binding the entire wood system of the tree together, the rays also give it a certain amount of its pattern. (When these rays separate, they are called checks.) As the tree ages, the sapwood be-

Fig. 1-3 *A dramatic example of mask carving and sculpture in this piece, by Dick Salazar. The dark wood is textured to define the coarseness of the hair and moustache. The brow line is run all the way across, giving the eyes definition and character.*

comes harder and ceases to serve as a transporting tube for the sap. It becomes the essential support for the tree and is referred to as *heartwood*. Heartwood is usually harder than sapwood, and there is generally a drastic color difference between the two.

Grain

The grain, whether it is close or open, can be an asset or a detriment depending on the design of a woodcarving. A long, thin, open-grained piece of wood would suffer a great loss of durability, but a short, stocky, close-grained piece might not be as attractive. An open-grained wood is decorative in itself.

Fig. 1-4 *Jar with a carved lid, about 8" high, by Dick Salazar. Formed from different patterns of wood into a parquet-type design, and then shaped into a circular container. The lid is fitted and carved with a flower pattern.*

Burls, knots, and checks (cracks) are all a part of growth patterns, and when applied to a simple design, they usually enhance the carving. However, these abnormalities in the wood also can work against a design if you have not taken care to incorporate them into it at the beginning of the project.

Grain is the result of the growth of fibers surrounding the food-carrying cells, comprising the rays. These fibers and the two layers that the tree grows seasonally—spring growth is a lighter wood and summer is darker—form the grain. The age-telling *tings*, the annual rings, are formed by both seasonal woods every year with variations based on the climate, environmental conditions, and moisture availability. These differences in the environment make

Fig. 1-5 *"Gold-finches in a Dogwood Tree," by Austin C. Burroughs. Some of the most breathtakingly lifelike bird carvings seen anywhere have been created by Burroughs, whose life-size, freestanding duck placed third in the prestigious World Competition at Salisbury, Maryland, this year. The show is sponsored by the Ward Foundation.*

Fig. 1-6 *"Blue Jay," carved and painted by Austin C. Burroughs.*

thicker or thinner rings. (Thinner, close grained rings are generally preferable for finer carving woods.) Knots or burls, odd colorations and markings from fires, and animal and insect damage are other environmental factors that make the wood unique.

Fig. 1-7 *Life-size, carved and painted duck by Austin C. Burroughs.*

Fig. 1-8 *Ironwood giraffe made by the Zuñi Indians has a close, tight grain. The hardness of the wood contrasts with the thin, graceful lines of the piece. (Courtesy, Cecil E. Lewis)*

As soon as a tree is cut down, it begins to dry. The rings contract from the moisture loss at different times and rates throughout the wood. Since the loss causes stress at these points and not at the other, wetter areas, the contracting wood causes checks and cracks. The rays are the weakest part of these rings, and this is where the checks usually occur.

Color

Nature provides an astounding array of wood colors. And what is even more fortuitous for the woodcarver

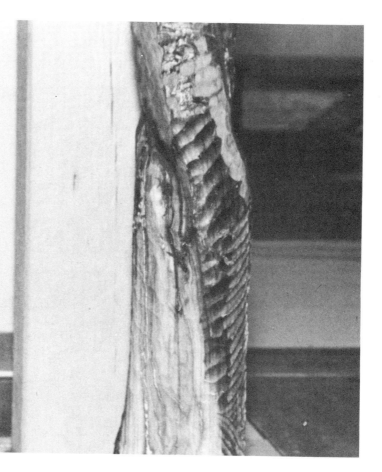

Fig. 1-9 *Designing a piece around both sapwood (the lighter wood) and heartwood (the darker, inner core) will result in great shadowing and contrast.*

is that every piece of wood, even within the same species, will vary in color intensity and pattern. Softwoods and hardwoods, as well as the medium-hard woods, share the same colors, so you do not have to select a particular type of wood for a particular design. Nature's palette extends from the creamy whites, beiges, and tans of basswood, pine, and butternut, to the pinkish tones of alder and maple, and the rich reddish-brown of cherry, to the opulent browns of mahogany and walnut, all the way through not only to ebony black, but to the startling exotic striations of zebrawood.

Hardwoods and Softwoods

Cabinetmakers and carpenters define hardwoods as the woods from deciduous, broad-leaved trees, and

Fig. 1-10 *This carved arm from an antique chair shows off the richness of cherry when used for furniture.*

softwoods from needle-bearing trees (conifers). The woods listed here are characterized by their degree of hardness to the carving tool and the knife blade, and not by their botanical or technical classification. Cedar is technically classified as a soft wood, even

Fig. 1-11 *Carved mahogany shelf.*

Fig. 1-12 *The outstanding grain pattern of mahogany shows clearly in this detail of the carved shelf front.*

though it is more durable than brittle Philippine mahogany, which technically is a hard wood.

The following woods are fairly common and available commercially, either at craft or hobby stores, hardware stores, lumberyards, or through mail-order companies (see List of Suppliers).

Alder: Alder is a pale pink to brownish-pink wood with an undistinguishable grain. These attributes are a plus if you want to finish the piece to look like another species. Darker, For example, to look like walnut, or yellowed to look like pine. The wood is medium hard for carving, but it does not damage or split easily.

Ash: Ash is a very hard wood frequently used for woodcarving mallets and tool handles. It is gray or brownish tinged with white and red. Ash finishes well, but it should be carved with the sharpest tools because the grain is open. It may split, but this is usually not a problem.

Basswood: Basswood is most similar to white pine, and some of its characteristics resemble cottonwood. The softness of the wood and the close grain give it the same tendency to split or damage if the tools used are not absolutely razor sharp. Although both basswood and pine are creamy white to deep beige, basswood usually lacks the more clearly defined grain of pine or the distinct pine odor.

Beech: Beech is a hard wood frequently used for tool handles or mallets. It is also frequently used for kitchen utensils, since it has no odor or taste after it has completely dried. Unless properly seasoned, beech checks more easily than most other woods of the same hardness. The color is white with reddish-brown tinges.

Birch: Birch is a hard wood with a moderately close grain. Because of the grain, it is nearly indistinguishable and varies in color from a creamy white to a light brown, sometimes with pink overtones. Birch is highly resistant to splitting while being worked. However, it does tend to check while seasoning. Because it finishes so well and takes a good polish, it is worth the extra care necessary during drying.

Butternut: Butternut is a soft, easy to carve wood with a pleasant creamy tan color. The grain pattern is moderate. The color is the main advantage of this wood. With patience, butternut carves well and makes an attractive finished piece. It tends to chip if it is worked too fast and too hard. The final result is worth the extra effort and time.

Cedar: Cedar is a popular wood for an initial try at whittling shapes or forms (as opposed to a more detailed piece). It is a medium-hard wood and can be brittle, so it is best to go slow with the cedar project to avoid splitting the wood. The end result is very rewarding for the extra effort. Because of its weathering and durability, cedar is an excellent choice for signs or pieces that will be placed outdoors and exposed to the elements. Its characteristic smell and its color variations from creamy pink to red with cream streaks make for a distinctive end product.

Cherry: Cherry is a medium-hard wood with a moderate to very close grain. It does not cut easily, but it finishes well and resists splitting. Shades vary from light to dark reddish browns. This is a popular wood for either carving or whittling free-form or detailed pieces. Cherry is often the choice for fine furniture makers because of its fine texture, color, and durability.

Cottonwood: Cottonwood is similar to basswood in that it is relatively soft and does not have a distinct grain. Both woods are creamy white to brown, although cottonwood has more of a gray tint to its creamy tones. Cottonwood is good for detail because it splits very little when being worked.

Cypress: Cypress is a medium-hard wood with a straight, close grain. It is often used for outside ornamentation or for decorative carvings for boats and houses. Cypress weathers well and is durable like redwood. The colors range from very light to deep browns with red tinges.

Elm (American): American elm is a medium-hard wood with a moderate grain pattern. The color varies from a light brown to a darker brown with reddish streaks. The pores are close, so the wood resists splitting. Elm is one of the more difficult woods to carve, but it finishes well.

Hickory: Hickory is hard to carve, but its moderate grain pattern and the brown and brownish-red tones make attractive form and abstract carvings. Hickory has been popular for years as a whittling wood (generally walking sticks with a minimum of detail). The pattern of the grain is complemented by the open pores. These open pores, however, allow rapid moisture loss, so checks and cracks are frequently a problem. Always season the stock well before starting.

Holly: Holly is a hard wood that is relatively difficult to carve. It is one of a number of woods, however, that darken with age and take on pleasing shadings. Holly has an indistinguishable grain. The color is yellowish white before it ages and deepens. With sharp tools, details are easily carved with little risk of splitting.

Ironwood: Ironwood is an extremely hard wood found in the Southwest. Because of its deep red and dark brown color, it is dramatic for simple, undetailed pieces. Heavy waxing using shoe wax produces a hard, beautiful luster. Razor-sharp tools and heavy mallets are necessary to cut into this wood, so it is not recommended for beginning projects.

Magnolia: Magnolia is a medium-hard wood that is fairly good for carving. It finishes well, and the pale green tone of the brown wood is a real conversation piece. The grain is not prominent and is close.

Mahogany (Cuban): Cuban Mahogany is a hard wood with a beautiful, rich color and an outstanding grain pattern. The color varies in tone from light brown to a deeper brown. This type of mahogany (not to be confused with "Philippine" mahogany, which is not a member of the mahogany family at all) is excellent for carving and it takes a beautiful finish. It has an open grain but is fairly resistant to splitting while being carved.

Mahogany (Honduran): Honduran mahogany is an easily carved, moderately hard wood. With its yellow/brown to deep red tones, it makes an interesting finished carving. Although the grain is open, the wood does not split easily.

Maple: Maple is a pinkish-beige to light reddish-brown wood with a close grain. It does not split easily although it is a medium-hard wood to carve. Maple is a beautiful wood for abstract pieces because it finishes so well and the grain is subtle but apparent.

Myrtle (California): Myrtle is a hard wood that has a warm golden-brown color. Some of the more exciting pieces have green tones in them. The grain is a moderate pattern, but it is the color that is the strong point. Although moderately hard to carve, it is not impossible with good, razor-sharp tools. The finish is also well worth the time and effort. The grain is close and the resistance to splitting is good.

Oak (American red): Oak has a well-defined grain and it does not split easily, but it is also very hard. The coarseness of the pores and its hardness make it almost impossible to whittle with any ease, but with properly sharpened tools, it carves beautifully. It also lends itself to form rather than details. Grayish-brown to light reddish-brown color variations, along with the coarse grain, make oak a readily identifiable wood.

Oak (American white): White oak, a hard, coarse-grained wood, is usually light gray in color but can have a yellowish/tan tone. Because of its pronounced pores and hardness, details may be difficult to carve, but with sharp tools, it carves beautifully.

Pecan: Pecan is a medium-hard wood that carves well, but it is difficult to whittle. It has open pores and a close, distinct grain. Like cherry, pecan is a reddish brown but with creamy overtones. Also like cherry, it is a highly prized wood for furniture.

Pine: Pine is perhaps the most common wood used by the beginning woodcarver for a first piece, either carved or whittled. The grain is closed, and with sharp tools, splitting can be kept to a minimum. Pine is soft, with color variations from white to a deep beige often in the same stock of wood.

Poplar: Poplar is a medium-hard wood that runs from yellow to yellow-brown. The grain is moderately visible, and it finishes well because of the close grain. It is popular for whittling because it cuts easily and resists splitting.

Redwood: Redwood is a popular wood for outdoor carvings, furniture, and sign plaques because it is weather-resistant. It is a moderately soft wood to carve, and it works well with hand tools. The wood is a deep reddish-brown and has a prominent grain pattern.

Sweet Gum: Sweet gum is a medium-hard wood with reddish to brownish tones. The grain is apparent but not prominent. Despite easy checking, sweet gum works and finishes well.

Walnut (American black): Black walnut, a personal favorite for both whittling and carving, is a hard wood, but because it is oily, it does not split easily. The close grain finishes beautifully with hand rubbing, and the light brown to deep purplish brown colors make for distinctive pieces. Little detail is necessary. It is the hardest and darkest of the three types of walnut usually available commercially.

Walnut (California and European): Both kinds of walnut are moderate in hardness and have an outstanding grain pattern on a tan to dark brown background.

Willow: Willow is a soft wood, easily carved, with a creamy color and no real distinguishable grain. It can be likened to basswood and cottonwood in that it works well, even for details, and finishes well. The grain is closed and resists splitting.

Exotic Woods

After you have tried and mastered a few pieces carved or whittled out of the "traditional" woods, you can try some of the more challenging ones. These woods are extremely hard to work with, but each has an outstanding grain and color, and the finished pieces can often be breathtaking for the inspired intermediate or advanced carvers.

Ebony: One of the hardest woods, ebony is deep black in color and has a close, indistinguishable grain. Ebony pieces can be burnished to a high luster, with a lovely gloss finish. Because of its extreme hardness, ebony resists splitting. However, it will tend to chip because of its brittleness. It should be carved only with the sharpest, strongest tools.

Lignum Vitae: Lignum Vitae is a good wood for tool handles and mallet heads because of its extreme hardness. It also makes elegant carved pieces. The color ranges from olive to dark brown with lighter streaks running throughout. The finish on this wood is spectacular. It burnishes beautifully and splits very little for such a hard wood.

Persimmon: Persimmon is a very hard wood with a distinct, prominent grain pattern. It is a rich brown with deeper stripes mottling the wood. Because of its close grain, persimmon resists splitting. Like all the woods in this list, it is difficult and slow carving. But it finishes so well and is so beautiful that it is well worth the effort.

Rosewood: Mixed browns, purples, and blacks make rosewood one of the most beautiful woods available. The grain is quite distinct with light and dark swirls and stripes. Rosewood does not split, but like other extremely hard woods, it is difficult to carve and tends to chip easily.

Satinwood: Satinwood is extremely hard to carve, but the golden hue gleams when finished to a high polish. The grain is close and only moderately apparent. This wood is worth the extra work for the pale golden cast. It resists splitting well.

Teak: Teak has a pronounced, well-defined grain that finishes well. It is definitely a hard wood, but it is not as difficult to carve as either rosewood or ebony. The wood is yellowish with darker yellow to brown streaks.

Zebrawood: Zebrawood, a hard wood, is popular because of its distinct stripes in yellow/beige to dark brown. It is very difficult to carve but uniquely beautiful when finished.

Woods to Avoid

It can be disappointing to spend time on woods that seem to thwart your efforts. Some woods aren't worth your investment of time and effort because they are soft, brittle, or have a high resin content:

Balsa: Balsa is so soft and with such an open grain that it damages easily from carving tools and even while handling it. Razor-thin, sharp blades are the only implements that work on this delicate wood. Balsa is white to pinkish tones. While it is a good wood for miniatures or small models, it is inappropriate for carving or whittling.

Chestnut: Checks are common in chestnut, and a sizeable piece of stock may be diminished considerably as you find checks throughout the interior. Chestnut is a medium-hard wood with a coarse grain. The gray to red-brown color is appealing, but the wood can be frustrating to work with.

Douglas Fir: A medium-hard wood, Douglas fir has such a wide grain, due to its resin canals, it tends to split along these weak spots fairly easily. The orange to red/brown color range finishes fairly well, but resin leaks can mar the finished surface and detract from the overall appearance.

Philippine "mahogany": This wood is not in the mahogany family, but because of its red to brown color similarity and its moderately open grain, it is often mistaken for genuine mahogany. Philippine mahogany tends to split and damage easily, especially if the tools used are not razor sharp. It is a medium-hard wood with a coarse grain, and it does not finish well.

Spruce: Spruce is a medium density, close-grained wood that, like Douglas fir, has resin canals that leak and split. It is beige to deep beige-brown. Although it can be worked, it is not worth the effort.

Seasoning Woods

Seasoning a felled log will prevent rapid and uneven moisture loss. If the log is properly seasoned, it will dry out without causing checks and cracks. Seasoning can be accomplished in several ways with good results. There are chemical soaks that smaller logs and cut stock can be placed in for several days or weeks, the time varying according to the type of wood.

Polyethylene glycol (PEG), available in hardware stores, is the most common wood soak used by woodworkers and woodcarvers. Woodcarvings should be worked or sawed to the rough size and shape of the finished piece before soaking. PEG is not inexpensive, so it is best to prepare the piece as close to the finished dimensions as possible. Dry woods must be presoaked in water, since the principles of PEG rely on water to gain entry to the wood. Green woods, if they are truly green do not have to be presoaked. The soaking time varies greatly from hard to soft woods and from thick to thin pieces. Drying times are available where PEG is purchased.

Using PEG-treated wood is better than using checked or cracked wood. It is better than green wood, but even PEG wood is not perfect. The solution will occasionally bleed from the wood if the finished piece is not sealed. Because its main function is to draw water to it, it will continue to absorb humidity if it is not sealed. The other drawback is the time involved, anywhere from a week or two to six to eight weeks. Of course, this time factor is put into better perspective when the artist considers that it can take

Fig. 1-13 *The rays and annual rings are apparent on this cherry log, where the wax has cracked. To prevent further checking, a new coating of wax should be applied.*

a year or two of air drying to accomplish the same feat PEG can accomplish in a few weeks.

Air drying is an alternative seasoning method. The main factor here is the possibility of too rapid loss of the moisture in the wood, which can lead to cracks and checks. To minimize this loss and the attendant problems of warpage and shrinkage, leave the bark on the log and coat the ends with paraffin.

Raising logs off the ground with air space all around them for good ventilation is ideal. They should also be sheltered from the sun. Turn the pieces to ensure even drying, and check the end sealant to be certain that it has not cracked or peeled off. If it has, replace it immediately. If a log or piece of cut stock has already begun to check yet is still relatively green, try the PEG method. Often this procedure will sufficiently shrink the cracks uniformly, and an otherwise unusable piece becomes usable again.

Kiln drying is the commercial method of drying lumber. It removes moisture quickly while controlling the moisture loss with pressure. Unless a small amount of carving wood is being purchased, it is quite costly to the average carver. Unfortunately, the process is rarely available to the individual woodcarver. However, most wood purchased from lumberyards has already been kiln-dried.

CHAPTER 2

Woodcarving and Whittling Tools

UNTIL you find your niche in woodcarving, begin with a moderately priced but high-quality set of tools with tempered-steel blades. Inexpensive tools will not have the same balance and feel in your hand, and they will not give the same performance. And after the enthusiasm that goes into choosing the perfect piece of wood and being inspired by a pattern or design, you may become discouraged to find that the tools break easily or won't hold an edge.

Too often, though, a new woodcarver will invest a great deal of money in tools that have either an arcane purpose or are unnecessary. The happy medium is to begin with a few good tools and occasionally buy an odd tool for an unusual piece or for experimentation. A beginner's set of carving tools contains six to twelve of the standard, most frequently used tools. A basic set costs about $20. Tools purchased separately usually are under $5 each.

Knives

Many woodcarvers feel that "real" woodcarving should employ only chisels, gouges, and mallets, and

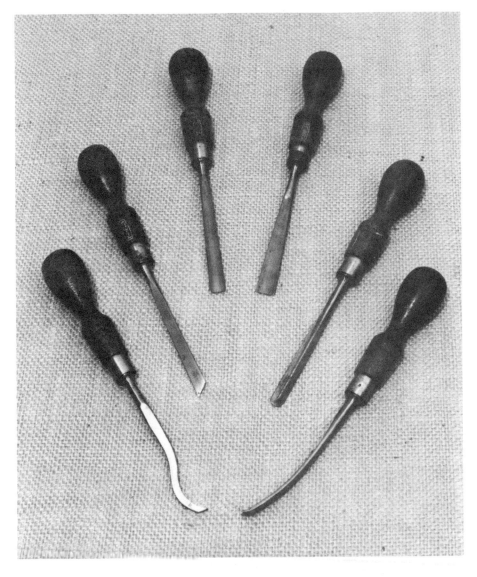

Fig. 2-1 *A basic set of woodcarving tools (clockwise from bottom left): bent chisel, $\frac{1}{4}''$ skew chisel, $\frac{3}{8}''$ straight gouge, $\frac{1}{2}''$ straight gouge, $\frac{5}{16}''$ V-tool, and $\frac{1}{4}''$ curved gouge.*

Fig. 2-2 *A basic set of knives, including a draw knife, sheepfoot, varied sheepfoot, and slant-tip.*

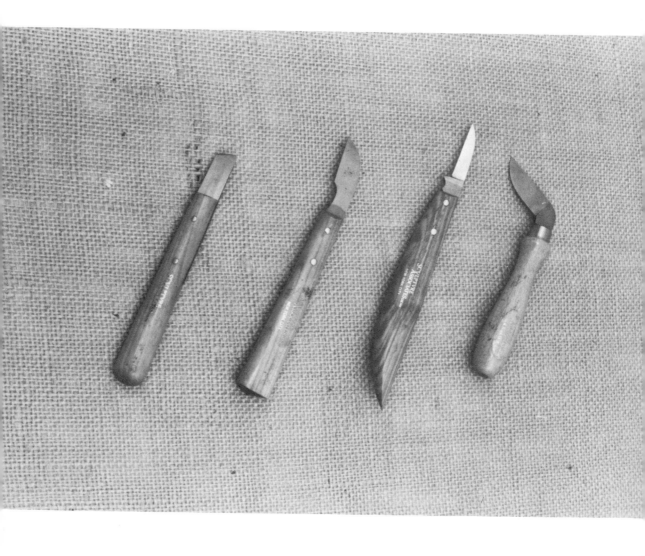

that knives are just for whittling, as though whittling were a lesser art. Functionally, however, knives can be more versatile than the tools made expressly for carving. Practicing with knives before learning to use chisels and mallets is tbe best introduction to wood-carving. Start with a good, sharp blade, as on a pocketknife, and a soft piece of wood like pine. This will give you a feeling for the grain, the softness or hardness of the wood, and the different textures that can be produced.

Carving knives can be used for whittling small hand-held pieces, for ornamental carving such as decorative moldings or friezes, or for classic chip carvings, where the wood is removed in wedge-shaped pieces. Chip-carving knives have short blades and light handles and are meant to be held in one hand. Because the point is the main part used for carving, it needs to be ground to its sharpest. Dull edges grab and gouge the wood haphazardly and damage the piece. Chip carving leaves a rough surface with rich texture, but it is uniform and the chip cuts are cleanly sliced.

A good sharp blade and point on a quality pocketknife can cover so many functions that it is often all many experienced carvers use. However, part of the enjoyment of carving and whittling is learning how to use various tools. Luckily, there are as many on the market as your budget will allow.

Fig. 2-3 *Close-up of the spear-point blade.*

Although there are many kinds of knives, most are variations on five basic types. The first three are frequently found on pocketknives:

Sheepfoot: The sheepfoot cutting edge is straight, and the back of the blade is heavy with a slight curve

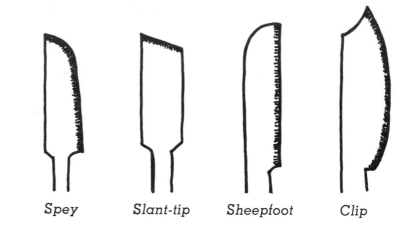

Fig. 2-4 *Knife blades.*

Spey   **Slant-tip**   **Sheepfoot**   **Clip**

to provide stability. If the blade gives easily, so might the wood. The clean cuts essential to chip carving would be ragged and uneven.

Spear Point: The spear point is the "penknife" blade found on pocket knives. Similar in shape to the sheepfoot, with the curved back ending in a sharp point at the tip, it is best used for cutting fine lines.

Clip Blade: For finer curved or straight lines and for hard-to-reach areas on small pieces, a good blade to have on hand is the clip blade. It has a long curved edge that comes to a pointed tip and is a good all-purpose blade.

Slant Tip: The main purpose of the slant-tip blade is to make deep or large cuts. It is also used for the same purpose as the sheepfoot—for chip carving and hardwood whittling. However, slant-tip knives are not as thick or sturdy as the sheepfoot, and they work best on softer woods.

Spey Tip: The spey tip is a good blade for curves and small areas. The shape of the blade is directly opposite that of the sheepfoot: The blade is curved and the back straight.

Beyond the five basic knife blades, there are slight variations on each in size, shape, and width. Many are longer with thinner blades for more specific line and curved carving. Others, such as chisel blades, are strong and stubby for heavy use. Curved handles and blades are handy for small hand-held pieces.

Chisels and Gouges

Chisels have a straight cutting edge, usually beveled on both sides, and are designed for cutting or chipping. A chisel may be bent, curved, spooned, or fish-tailed, but the cutting edge is always flat. The skew-tip chisel has an angled cutting edge, and it, too, may be bent, spooned, curved or fish-tailed.

Gouges are double-edged blades similar to chisels, but their cutting edges are curved. They are identified by an arbitrary number denoting curvature of the blade. Lower numbers are flatter curves and higher numbers are deeper curves. All widths have the same *relative* curve, although the actual radii may vary. V gouges are V-shaped, two-sided chisels that are usually angled from 60 to 90 degrees. As with other gouges, they come straight or curved.

A Beginner's Repertoire

Some good starting tools are:

$\frac{1}{4}''$ *Skew Chisel:* The skew chisel, which is straight with an angled cutting edge, is good for deep diagonal cuts and decorative borders and edgings.

Fig. 2-5 *A basic set of large woodcarving tools, including straight gouges and chisels and the V-tool.*

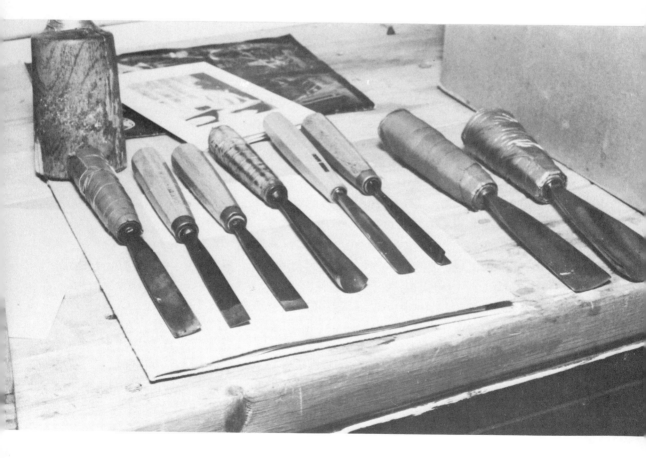

$\frac{3}{8}''$ *Straight Gouge:* This gouge is a sturdy beginner's tool for use with a mallet or hand pressure. The moderately curved blade edge helps prevent gouging while you learn the proper pressure to apply.

$\frac{1}{2}''$ *Straight Gouge:* This tool works well for bosting (rough cutting) and for making other big cuts when used with a mallet. The slight curvature allows leeway for error in striking pressure without running the blade directly into the wood.

$\frac{1}{4}''$ *Curved Gouge:* This gouge and the bent gouge (same as curved, only the curve of the tool is much greater) are excellent for preliminary background cutting in relief carving and for incised carving, where the texture is as important to the design as the design itself.

$\frac{5}{16}''$ *V Tool:* Also called a parting tool, this is best for line carving, where only small, thin pieces of wood are to be removed at a time. It is also good for removing small amounts of wood from sharply angled areas of the piece, or wherever you want to maintain a sharp, crisp line.

Interchangeable Handles and Blades

Chisels and gouges are often sold without handles so that the carver can select a handle that is best suited for his or her own hand. The blades can be mounted and sharpened professionally where you buy them, or you can do it yourself.

Handles come in several shapes. Some are barrel-shaped and curved slightly to fit the hand. One popular type of handle is barrel-shaped with a flat plane on the bottom to prevent the tool from rolling on

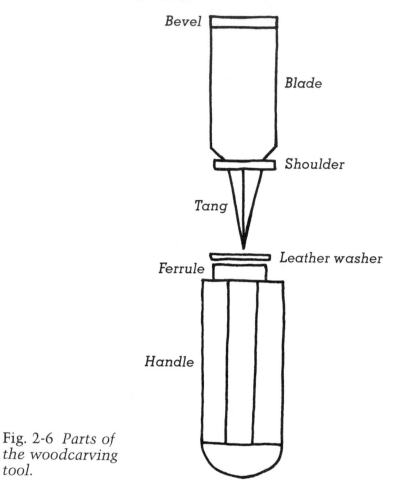

Bevel

Blade

Shoulder

Tang

Leather washer

Ferrule

Handle

Fig. 2-6 *Parts of
the woodcarving
tool.*

the work table. Others have several flat-planed areas. The rule of thumb here is if the handle feels good in your hand, buy it.

The most important part of fitting blades to handles is that it be done perfectly straight so that you can gauge an angle or a straight cut. A blade that angles out of a perfect handle will not perform efficiently. The handle should be drilled with a bit the size of the narrowest part of the tang. Drill the full

depth of the tang, and then redrill to widen the hole.
When the tang can be inserted by hand halfway into
the handle, grip the tool firmly in a vise and tap
firmly and evenly until the handle is on securely.
Tap the handle, not the blade, to prevent damaging
the blade. To allow for loosening with use, place a
leather washer between the shoulder and ferrule of
the handle. When the blade begins to loosen, simply
tap the handle until the blade is once again firmly
in place. If you have fitted the handle properly, these
adjustments are usually necessary only every several
years or after much hard use.

X-Acto makes a handle with interchangeable blades
in many handy shapes and sizes for hand-carving
without striking with a mallet. With only a few handles and many blades, you can do all types of carving
and need only minimum storage space for the tools.
An added bonus is that the blades can be popped in
and out as needed without having to sharpen each
one as you use it. The limitation, however, is that
the tool will not perform well under great pressure,
such as that resulting from being struck with a mallet. The blades are not as sturdy as those in single-
purpose tools, but are adequate for hobby work.

Mallets

Mallets are relatives of hammers; their sole purpose is to strike another tool. The head of the mallet
is usually made of a hardwood such as beech, rosewood, or hickory. Experienced woodcarvers have their
own preferences as to weight, which varies from 6
to 40 ounces, and diameters, which vary from 2 to
7 inches. Obviously, larger, harder woods require
larger, heavier mallets to provide the necessary force.

Fig. 2-7 *Hardwood mallet. The head is made of ash.*

Fig. 2-8 *Wrap the mallet handle with tape for a better grip. The tape will also keep the mallet from cracking.*

A recent newcomer on the market is the urethane mallet, which is hard but pliable and practically indestructable.

Clamps, Vises, and Wood Screws

Many types, shapes, sizes, and weights of clamping devices are available to the woodcarver. The size of the clamp or vise is determined by the size and shape of your project.

If the piece is to be incised-carved, simple clamps will hold the flat board in place while the rough work is being done. However, if the wood stock is to be carved in the round, the clamps would interfere. Instead, you could use a long bench screw, or wood screw, to hold the piece securely. A bench screw is a long, winged-head screw that passes through the workbench into the base of the wood to be carved.

A common vise attached to the workbench is good for in-the-round pieces, but the pieces must be rotated frequently to make sure you are carving all areas evenly, and the wood is not marred by the pressure being applied for long periods.

If the clamp or vise you choose for a particular piece is too cumbersome to move, or if it gets in your way too frequently, it has defeated its purpose. Only large pieces need to be secured to a workbench.

The Workbench

One commercially available workbench that is excellent for most types of carving, whether hand-held or clamped, is Black and Decker's Work-Mate, which costs about $110. This convenient all-in-one table is also portable. The vertical vise can hold large pieces of wood and is sturdy enough to withstand the pres-

Fig. 2-9 *C-clamp.*

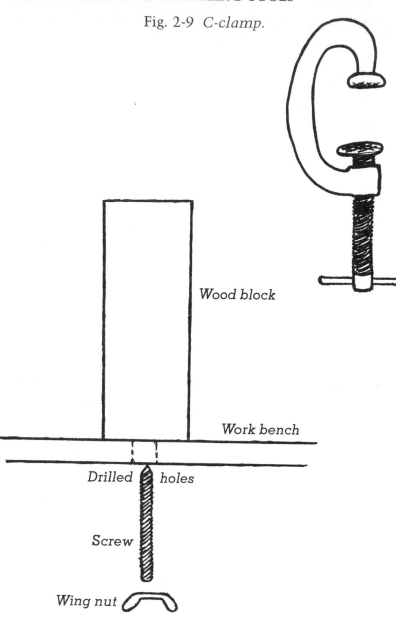

Wood block

Work bench

Drilled holes

Screw

Wing nut

Fig. 2-10 *Wood (bench) screw. The screw is put through a drilled hole in the bench and into the wood, then tightened with a wing nut.*

sure of mallet work. Whichever type of work surface you choose, the main prerequisite is that it must allow you the confidence to know that the work will not shift under pressure. If the piece moves unexpectedly, a good, solid blow that is misplaced will damage the work.

Files and Rifflers

Files and rifflers are small, sharp-toothed tools that are used to smooth hard-to-reach areas. The teeth must be kept free of small wood chips in order to work efficiently. Files come in flat, round, and half-round and, like sandpaper, range from coarse to fine. Rasps are files with large, pointed teeth used primarily for rough shaping.

Spokeshave

A small spokeshave, a blade with a handle at each end, is useful for shaping curved and rounded areas. In fact, you may find that a spokeshave works faster and better on curves than any of the conventional carving tools. Always use it with the grain to avoid removing large strings of wood. The blade should be kept razor sharp. The best way to use a spokeshave is to push it forward lightly, bring it back, and move forward a little at a time. This maneuver will prevent removal of too much wood.

Power Tools

Many purists cringe at the thought of power tools being used for woodcarving. However, removing the waste areas from large pieces can be so time-consuming that the carver can lose interest in the work before it is ever really started. Woodcarving is a rest-

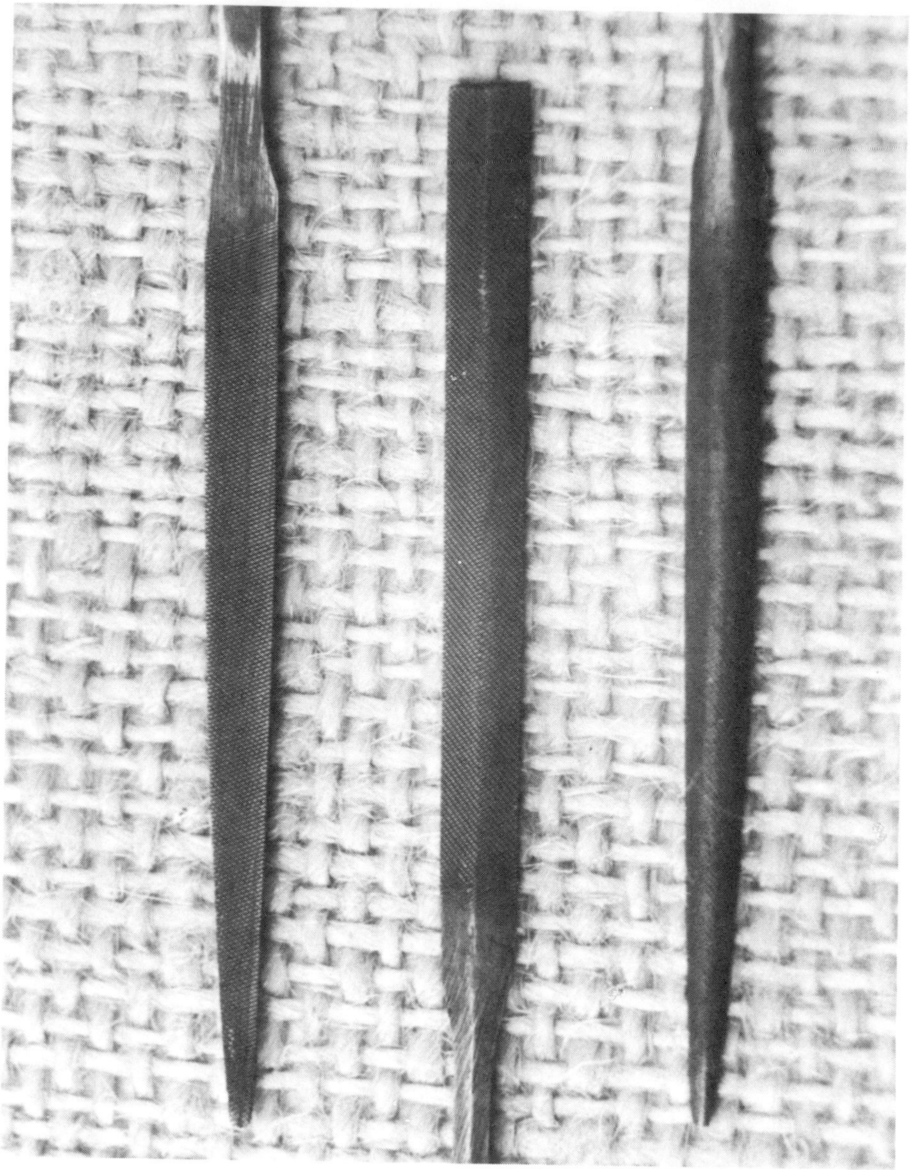

Fig. 2-11 *Fine-toothed rifflers, 3″
to 4″ long.*

Fig. 2-12 *A rasp and small rifflers.*

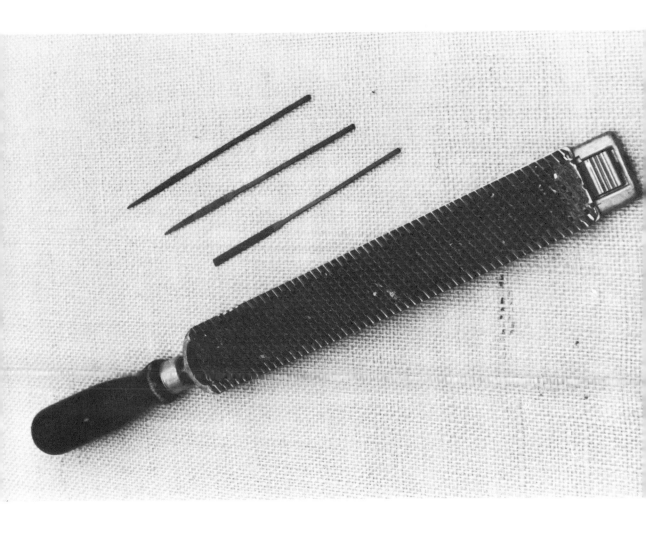

Fig. 2-13 *Wood planes and (right) spokeshave.*

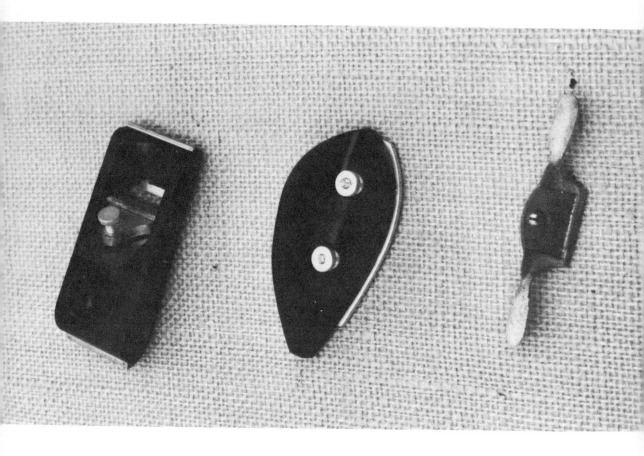

ful, creative art, and the rapport you will develop with the wood will not be diminished just because you use a labor-saving device. Power tools can save you work and allow you to spend your time on the actual carving.

Bandsaws are useful for cutting angled and curved shapes. The saw blade is thin and travels down and around in a circular motion. The blade has a slight give to it, but it is not as flexible—nor is it used for the same purpose—as a jigsaw or scroll saw. The main use for a bandsaw in woodcarving is to shape a large piece of wood before hand-carving it. Bandsaws come in a variety of sizes and weights and are available in various price ranges.

Bandsaws

The conventional portable power drill is specifically for making holes in wood. Holes less than one-quarter inch in diameter are *drilled.* Holes larger than one-quarter inch are *bored.* Despite these technical woodworking terms, a hole is still a hole. Portable drills are useful, but a drill press is a better tool for the woodcarver because boring holes is a time-consuming process. Like bandsaws, drill presses come in a variety of sizes and weights.

Drill Presses

Tool Sharpening

Every woodcarver should learn how to sharpen tools, since razor-sharp tools are essential for clean, clear cuts and to prevent gouging and splitting the wood.

Although fine tempered-steel blades will hold an edge much longer than blades made of an inferior grade of steel, you will still have to sharpen them. Most mail-order houses and hardware stores usually have facilities for fitting and sharpening blades. But

Fig. 2-14 *Beveled tool edges ready to be sharpened.*

becoming proficient with a sharpening stone is a good skill to acquire because it will save you money and time.

Most tools are professionally ground to a beveled edge, even if they are not sharpened to a fine carving edge. The initial beveled edge is carefully formed on a grinding wheel. If a tool edge becomes chipped during use, have it reground by a professional. If it is not reground properly, the blade will not hold an edge.

For sharpening your tools after grinding them, you will need two sharpening stones, one coarse and one fine. Many hardware stores and mail-order craft houses carry two-sided—coarse and fine—stones. Carborundum is a well-known coarse stone that, used with No. 10 motor oil as a lubricant, will sharpen the dullest edges. The coarseness of the surface abrades the metal to a keen edge, and the oil keeps these abrading pores of the stone clear. If too much metal debris accumulates on the surface, the stone will not sharpen well. To unclog the pores of the stone, saturate it with a solvent such as liquid dishwashing detergent.

A ground edge alone is not sufficiently sharp for wood-cutting purposes. It is a single step in a multistep process. To sharpen a straight-edge tool after it has been ground to a beveled edge.

Straight-Edge Tools

1. Note whether the chisel should be beveled on one side only or on both sides equally. Note, too, the angle of the bevel; it is difficult to change simply by rubbing the blade on an oilstone, since the purpose of the stone is to *sharpen* the cutting edge, not to form it.

2. Load the stone by applying lubricant and rub it thoroughly into the pores (Fig. 2-15). Mineral oil, No. 10 motor oil, or liquid dishwashing detergent will work perfectly.

3. In one hand, hold the tool steady to maintain the proper angle, and with your other hand apply even pressure as you rub the blade back and forth over the stone (Figs. 2-16 and 2-17). This is called *whetting,* and the sharpening stone is called a *whetstone.*

4. Periodically check the edge of the blade for sharpness. To do this, rub one finger down the side of the tool and across the edge of the blade. You will feel a definite roughness if the tool is sufficiently sharpened. This roughness is called the *burr.*

5. Turn the tool over and rub gently back and forth to remove the wire burr edge (Fig. 2-21). Turn as necessary to eliminate the largest portions of the burr.

6. Repeat the entire sharpening process using the finer stone. This *honing* will remove the rest of the burr.

Many "classic" woodcarvers strop the edge of their tools after sharpening. This is believed to give the edge an even finer finish. A strop is a long, thick piece of leather glued onto a piece of wood. Some carvers use the same type of strop that barbers used to use for shaving-blade sharpening. Cover the strop with a very fine grade of pumice or emery powder and draw the tool edge across it. Work in one direction to maintain the proper angle on the strop.

If a tool becomes dull after some use, it can be honed to a keen edge by sharpening it on the fine

Fig. 2-15 *A fine sharpening stone loaded and ready.*

Fig. 2-16 *The two-handed grip for tool sharpening.*

Fig. 2-17 *Maintaining the angle to keep the edge even.*

stone and then stropping. If the edge is worn from heavy use, you must first grind the edge and proceed with each step. Grinding is usually necessary only about once a year, and then only after heavy use. Honing can be done frequently to keep a sharp edge.

Chisels and Gouges

Chisels are always sharpened the same way, regardless of whether they are square or skew. However, the curved edge of a gouge makes sharpening on a conventional stone difficult. For gouges, you must use stones that are shaped to accommodate the curves and angles. These are called *slips,* and they come in coarse to fine grades. The same sharpening rules apply with these stones as with the flat ones.

Stropping a curved edge takes a little more patience than when dealing with a straight-edge tool. The old-time leather strop without the wood backing will curve to accommodate the edge if the tool is held near the edge of the leather and pulled downward to force the leather into the curve.

When sharpening a V tool (parting tool), use a knife-edged slip and sharpen the inside of the edge. Using this kind of slip care and patience. If the edge is not sharpened properly, a spike on the point will result, and the V tool will not work efficiently.

After taking the time and effort to grind, whet, hone, and strop your tools, it seems ludicrous to simply bunch them together, unprotected from one another, in a drawer or to be left on a bench top. The fine edges damage easily, since all are equally sharp and fine-honed. They will soon dull if left to rub against each other or against other tools. A pocketed canvas roll will protect them and keep them in easy reach.

CHAPTER 3

Tool Grips, Wood Cuts and Techniques

BECAUSE wood is an organic material made up of bundles of fairly straight, even rows of fibers, it will cut cleanly if you work with the grain and roughly if you work against it. The grain can be approached from different angles, but working against it will almost always gouge the wood. Most woods have a readily identifiable grain direction, but it is not always predictable. By learning the basic hand grips and wood cuts that are used with the different woodcarving tools, you will be able to work effectively with the wood rather than against it. The grips and cuts are not difficult to learn, and once mastered, they will allow you to achieve the best results with the minimum of wear and tear on your nerves, the wood, and the tools.

Knife Grips for Carving and Whittling

Draw Grip

The most common grip for whittling, especially on softwood, is the draw grip (Fig. 3-1). The knife is held high on the palm and grasped tightly with the fingers. The thumb rests on the wood to help control the movement of the blade against it. The blade is drawn toward the carver, giving the added control

53

Fig. 3-1 *The draw grip.*

for either short or long cuts. Put a Band-Aid on your index finger at the pressure point to help prevent blisters during long sessions.

Forehand Grip   The forehand grip (Fig. 3-2) is the most common grip when removing large amounts of wood. It involves holding the knife in a clenched fist, with the blade facing away from the body. Because you will have little control stopping the blade in midcut, al-

Fig. 3-2 *The fore-hand grip.*

ways make these cuts away from the body to prevent injury.

The thumb-pointer grip (Fig. 3-3) is similar to the forehand grip, but the knife is held in a clenched fist and pushed away from the body. The thumb of the other hand controls the knife blade to enable a more controlled movement. Most carvers use this grip when making short cuts that require maximum control.

Thumb-Pointer Grip

Fig. 3-3 *The thumb-pointer grip.*

This grip is also good where you must make a deep cut in a precarious place.

Dagger Grip   The dagger grip (Fig. 3-4) is used for deep slicing cuts. Because this grip gives little control, use it only with a secured piece of wood. The knife is then pulled across or parallel to the body. This is a heavy-handed grip, so slips are not easily fixed. The knife is literally

Fig. 3-4 *The dag-
ger grip.*

held like a dagger, blade tip facing down drawn toward the body.

Pen Grip

The pen grip (Fig. 3-5) is excellent for fine detailing
or outlining work. The blade is held between the
fingers like a pen. The control and pressure comes
from the other fingers on the backside of the blade.
This is another potentially dangerous grip because

Fig. 3-5 *The pen grip.*

the fingers are placed so close to the blade. Care must be taken both with fingers and wood.

Basic Knife Cuts

Basic cuts, like the hand grips, can be varied to suit your hand and your needs. Many are actually combinations of two or more cuts. As you practice these basics, the variations and control will come more easily and naturally. These basic cuts are also applicable to chisels. In fact, they have been adapted for knife-blade use from chisel use—although knife-blade enthusiasts might disagree as to who borrowed from whom.

The stop cut (Fig. 3-6), the most basic of the basics, is made by cutting across the wood at a right angle from where the actual carving cut is to be made. This cut ensures that the knife will not run beyond

Stop Cut

Fig. 3-6 *The stop cut.*

where you want it to stop. When made properly, this cut acts as a limitation groove and prevents later cuts from ripping and removing large splinters of wood.

The stop cut is made with the tip of the blade at whatever depth the design calls for. Some artists make these cuts an essential part of the overall detail, while others leave them outside the boundaries of the design, to be removed later. In essence, they are only temporary guiding lines.

Wedge or Notch Cut

The wedge cut (Fig. 3-7) is a versatile cut that can be made with either the tip of the blade or the entire blade edge. This cut is most often used with chisels, or where it is necessary to remove rough wood. The wood is cut at an angle to the depth dictated by the design or wood texture. Then it is repeated on the opposite side, using the same angle and depth. The "V" of the wood is removed and the process repeated to remove large pieces of excess wood.

The wedge cut can also be used as a decorative border in itself. These cuts must be clean and crisp, done with an extremely sharp blade to slice the fibers rather than mash them. For maximum control and to be sure that you are applying the proper pressure, use the draw grip.

Back Cut

Back cuts are made after the stop cuts that outline and define the boundaries for the knife cuts. These are perpendicular to the stop cuts, and they are made on the waste side of the wood and merely outline further the limitations of the cuts. Back cuts are usually made only when the design calls for a raised surface. This is more of a carving-tool (such as the

Fig. 3-7 *The notch or wedge cut.*

gouge) technique that can be adapted for whittling purposes.

Saw Cut

The saw cut is good for detail and for removing small areas. The trick with the "sawing" method is to apply light pressure and let the sharpness of the blade do the work. With the blade flat against the wood, saw it back and forth until the proper depth is reached.

Beginning woodcarvers often saw the blade so deeply or with so much force that it becomes wedged in the wood. To remove it, try to back the knife gently out of the wood. If there appears to be a danger of splitting the wood, use another sharp blade to cut the other one out. If you are using a folding-blade pocketknife, be careful that the blade does not fold back on your fingers as you apply force.

Tip-Drill Cut

The tip-drill cut involves only the tip of the knife. It is simply a method of drilling a hole into or through the wood. The tip is forced into the wood and turned until the correct depth and circumference is reached. This cut, like all others, requires a razor-sharp blade. Otherwise, the blade will rip at the wood as it is rotated rather than cut a clean hole. This can be a disaster if the hole is integral to the design.

Grips for Chisels and Gouges

The basic grips for woodcarving tools are the same for both chisels and gouges. Many of the holds are similar to the grips for handling knives. The basic difference is that woodcarving tools are used either with two hands or with a one-handed grip while the other holds the mallet for striking. The size and hardness of the wood determine which grips to use. Most woodcarvers prefer gouges over chisels because of their ease of handling and their flexibility against the wood. A gouge's curved edge will not allow as deep a bite as a chisel will, and that allows greater flexibility.

When a cut is made with a perfectly square chisel, there is little margin for error. If the edge of the tool is placed incorrectly, of if it is hit with too much

Fig. 3-8 *Working* with *the grain.*

Fig. 3-9 *Making a shallow cut with a gouge.*

Fig. 3-10 *Running the gouge upward to remove chips smoothly
without gouging the wood.*

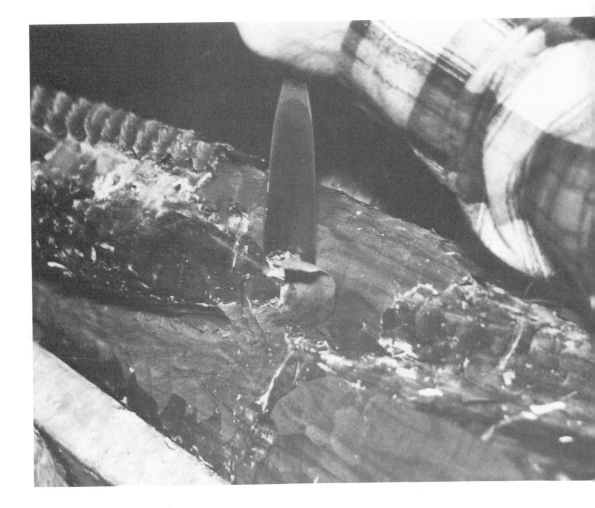

force, it will dig deeper. On the other hand, if a tool with a curved edge is struck too hard, it will tend to run upward, safely out of the wood.

For the maximum control, the tool should be held with both hands. The hand grasping the handle provides the pressure, and the other (grasping from the top of the tool, below the other hand) provides the control (see Fig. 3-11). This is important when doing delicate or fine-lined work. The guiding hand can actually restrain the tool if it is about to gouge the wood. The correct grasp is actually a normal one, and most carvers become comfortable with it after just a little practice.

Two-Handed Grip

The two-handed grip (Figs. 3-11 and 3-12) is the most common grip used without a mallet. One hand grasps the handle about midpoint, and the other hand is nearer the blade to guide the edge. Pressure is exerted by the top hand while a slight downward pressure from the lower hand provides stability. The angle of the tool to the wood should be ascertained before beginning the pressure to prevent cuts either too deep or at the wrong position in the wood. For fine-lined areas, where fine control is essential, the top hand should exert a gentle force, while the other hand grips the lower part of the tool like a pen. The upper hand on the handle helps to guide the tool and to provide pressure.

Pen Grip

The pen grip (see Fig. 3-5) allows the most control and the least pressure. It is best used for fine detail or for finishing another cut. The tool is held like a pen and the blade guided and pushed. This is a finishing grip and not a grip for large amounts of work.

Fig. 3-11 *The two-handed grip on the chisel.*

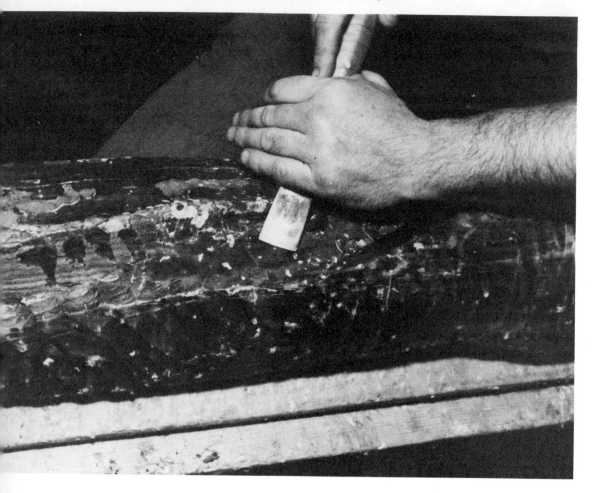

Fig. 3-12 *Hand pressure guides
the blade in the two-handed grip.*

The pen grip is awkward because the tool is held near the blade with the balance above the hand. The weight distribution is hard on the hand for long periods, but for small detail and fine work, the pen grip is quite useful.

The jeweler's grip resembles the grip a jeweler uses with an engraving tool. It is sometimes also referred to as the engraver's grip. The tool is grasped in the hand with the first finger extended just behind the blade. The thumb and other fingers hold the tool just below the handle, depending on the size of the tool. The handle is held firmly in the palm. This grip is good for running cuts, where control is necessary.

Jeweler's Grip

The mallet grip (Fig. 3-13) is used with a mallet. The tool is grasped at about midpoint, depending on its size and the size of your hand, or slightly lower. Before striking, place the tool at precisely the correct angle to be cut. Raise the mallet a few inches from the tool-handle end, and tap with light pressure. After you gain experience and know how much force is necessary to make the appropriate depth of cut, you can raise the mallet higher or strike more forcefully. It is best to start gradually and work up to this. This allows a gradual removal of the wood, instead of "chunks," which can cause costly mistakes.

Mallet Grip

Using a Mallet

Striking with a mallet is a technique that seems to be simple, yet it requires some skill. The tool should normally be struck by the mallet only from a very short distance. If the mallet is drawn back from the tool handle more than a few inches, the

Fig. 3-13 *The mallet grip.*

Fig. 3-14 *The head of the mallet is poised above the gouge handle, about to strike it.*

chances are good the mallet will miss the handle, or worse, hit only a glancing blow and chip a hunk from the wood. The force of the strike can vary depending on the type of wood, but the distance should not.

If you are right-handed, try holding the mallet in your left hand. Sometimes you will have to switch hands in order to get into a hard-to-reach area. Becoming ambidexterous can be of immeasurable help when the need arises. It is a good idea to practice on scrap stock.

When the tool is to be struck with a mallet, it is held in the hand with the fingers around the handle, the thumb closest to the top to be struck. It should be firmly grasped, yet the body should be flexible to move with the blow. Several short, light taps are preferable to heavy ones, especially when you are first learning how to handle the mallet. The important rule when striking with a mallet is always to strike with the tool facing away from the body. It seems common sense, but many a carver has unwittingly aimed at himself instead and slipped. Whenever dealing with force and sharp instruments, be cautious and careful.

Woodcarving Cuts

Bosting (Rough Cutting)

Bosting, sometimes called rough cutting, because it is the first step of roughing out the basic shape, entails cutting off the bulk of the wood that is not a part of the design.

After bosting out the stock, basic cuts can be made in combination with the grips used on chisels and gouges. As work progresses and you become more relaxed with the tools and wood, you can vary and combine these cuts, personalizing them to suit your designs.

The stop cut used with carving tools is similar to the stop cut used with knives (see Fig. 3-6). The purpose is also the same—to prevent the tool from running out of control. The stop cut is an outlining cut that makes a border for the carver to run the tool up to. It also prevents the wood from splitting as a result of running too deeply under the grain. Chisels and skews are generally used for straight cuts. For curved lines, use the appropriate gouge. Stop cuts are essential to maintaining the design when doing incised carving. These outlines protect the borders and give the design a straight, clean appearance.

Stop Cut

The running cut is best accomplished with the jeweler's grip if the tool and the piece are small and the cut is shallow. Use the two-handed grip if the piece is large and the cut is deep. The tool is grasped firmly, and with a continuous motion, guided with even force through the wood. The purpose of this cut is trimming and for doing the incised areas of a piece. It is one of the main cuts used for incised-carved plaques.

Running Cut

The wedge cut is a heavier, deeper version of the running cut. Use the mallet grip or the two-handed grip, depending on the tool and the size of the piece. When used in conjunction with the stop cut, the wedge is the most commonly used cut to remove thin to moderate slim wedges of wood. Tool blades must be razor sharp to make clean, smooth cuts and prevent gouging and splitting the wood. The angle of the tool should be assessed well before it is struck or pushed, to be sure the wedging is not too deep. Otherwise, it might splinter the wood. Sometimes the novice will angle too deeply and embed the tool

Wedge Cut

in the wood. It is best to rock the tool to try to remove it. If this doesn't work, use another tool to cut it out, cutting cautiously from the opposite direction.

Chip Carving

Chip carving, a simple and easy method of beginning carving, is one of the oldest forms of carving and involves only a single knife. It is so named because of the wedge-shaped chips that are removed from the wood, usually in geometric patterns. The design is drawn on the surface in pencil, then the triangular cuts are made, angling the sides to meet at a recessed point in the middle of the cut. Chip-carving knives must be razor sharp to make the wedges clean and precise. The beginning carver usually finds chip carving a rewarding first project because of the ease of the technique, and because of the speed with which projects can be completed. Chip carving is excellent for decorating drawer-front borders or door panels, or smaller items such as trays, bookends, and trivets. Softer woods are the best choices.

Incised Carving

Incised carving involves cutting grooves on the surface of the wood to form a pattern or design. The grooves can be made either with a gouge or with a knife blade, cutting down one bevel and then the other. The grooves are not necessarily triangular as in chip carving, but they usually form a U or a V shape uniformly throughout the piece. With practice, a veiner or parting tool can be used in one motion to create a perfect groove. This technique is more difficult than it looks, so practice first on scrap stock. Stop cuts should be made around the borders, but don't make them too deep or they may alter or interfere with the design.

Incised *line* carving is the simpler version of the same method. Grooves are made, but they are not as broadly dished, and the designs tend to be simpler as well. These thin grooves outline a picture or lettering while the background remains the same depth. Incised line carvings are the same as wood-block prints. On a woodcut, however, the background picks up the ink and the grooves produce a "negative" picture effect.

Relief Carving

Relief carvings fall into several classifications. First is high relief, where the background is deeply recessed from the carved foreground. Although it is not three-dimensional, it is similar to sculpture. Second is moderate relief, where the background is clearly recessed, but the foreground is almost equally prominent in depth as the base. Third is low relief, or bas-rclicf, which has a slightly raised look. Many incised carvings become low relief when the artist simply removes the background. Fourth is cameo-carving. Cameo-carved pieces have only the slightest differences in depth and height. Coins and medallions are good examples of this slight relief form. Many artists prefer to use combinations of relief forms to define perspective and add interest, expecially to high-relief pieces. A shallow background defines a higher foreground and eliminates a two-dimensional, flat look.

Intaglio

Intaglio carvings are just the opposite of relief. the main form or design is recessed instead of raised, with the background high and the design low or carved

Fig. 3-15 *This carved cherry chair is a beautiful example of relief carving.*

out. Wax seals and butter molds are the most common examples of this art form. If wax or clay were to be pressed against the surface of intaglio carvings, a relief carving would be the result. Many artists use this very method to determine if the depth of design is accurate or if more wood needs to be cut away.

Carving-in-the-Round

Carvings in-the-round, or direct carving, are three-dimensional. In effect, they are wood sculptures. This is generally considered to be the most difficult form of carving simply because more wood is removed and proper proportions are essential. Realistic wood carvings, such as bird or decoy carvings, which are accurate in every detail can be frustrating to the beginner because they require a great deal of skill to perfect. Wood carvings in-the-round can be carved with tools or whittled.

CHAPTER 4

Wood Finishes and Applications

JUST as you must balance the color and texture of the wood with your design, the finish you choose should also be weighed against these three elements. So, in a way, finishing in woodcarving is similar to beginning.

Most woods are admired for their appearance *after* the finish has been applied. Teak and walnut, for example, have a rich and highly distinguishable grain pattern that is at its intense best only when viewed through a finish. A clear or penetrating finish may be all that is needed for these types of woods, but with a pine or basswood you may want to use a stain. Stains can bring out an otherwise dull grain and add a new dimension to unadorned, "plain" woods.

Finishing is also a way to preserve your efforts and add durability to a woodcarving. Because wood is porous, it collects dirt and dust, which can discolor and dull the finish. It also can absorb moisture from the air and oil from handling the piece, and both can cause the wood to split and check. The proper finish will help prevent this.

Most wood-finishing products are made for furniture finishing and refinishing or for wood floors.

Because heavy use and subsequent durability are not factors with woodcarvings, choose a finish for other attributes—ease of application, drying time, and cost, and whether you want a gloss or matte finish.

This chapter discusses the basic products and materials that are most readily available at craft-supply and hardware stores or at lumberyards (see also List of Suppliers). The methods of application for each type of finish are also discussed. The surface of the piece must be sanded smooth and any checks or cracks filled and sanded before applying any finish.

Preparing the Wood

Sanding

Sanding is the essential first step in finishing a woodcarving. But how much sanding you do is up to you. Folk carvings, whittlings, and some contemporary wood pieces retain the tool marks as an integral part of the overall design. Other works, depending on the type of wood, are sanded glass smooth and polished to a high gloss. Often you will select a finish that lies somewhere in between.

Sandpaper comes in varying grades of abrasiveness, from coarse to extra fine. The higher the number of the grit, the coarser the paper. Always begin with a coarse grit and proceed to finer grits. To sand smooth, flat surfaces, attach a piece of sandpaper to a block of wood. For curved or odd-angled forms, wrap a piece of sandpaper around a wooden dowel or pencil to get into tightly curved or angled areas.

Water-base stains and finishes tend to raise the grain of the wood when they are applied. To prevent this, wet the piece slightly and allow it to dry thoroughly. Then sand the fuzz smooth. Use a fine-grit sandpaper and sand with, not across, the grain for the best finish.

Another method of smoothing that works well on detailed or curved carvings is steel-wooling. The fine filaments of metal shave minute pieces of wood and smooth it. As with sandpaper, progress from coarse to fine until you attain the desired finish.

A tack rag, available commercially, will remove minute dust particles and residue left after sanding or steel-wooling. Tack rags are impregnated with varnish, oil, and water, and with proper storage they will stay permanently damp.

Filling Cracks and Checks

Since wood is organic, every piece will differ in grain pattern, color, and imperfections. One imperfection is a check, or crack. Some woodcarvers use checks as an integral part of the design to offer contrast between the smooth, light area and the natural darkness of the check.

Others prefer to fill these naturally occurring flaws with a wood filler or with splinters and sawdust of the same wood. The choice is individual and varies from piece to piece. Filling the checks and cracks need not be done until you are ready to finish the piece. Examine it to see if the check adds or detracts from the design. If you decide to fill the crack, several commercial wood putties are available.

Plastic Wood, which is ready to use straight from the can, is probably the most popular type of filler. It comes in various wood colors, is easy to apply, and sets in a relatively short time. Force the Plastic Wood into the crack or check with a putty knife. If the check is deep, apply the filler in small amounts, allow each application to dry, then fill again. Repeat the applications until the check is full.

When using a wood filler, be careful not to smear it around the check. If you block the pores around

Fig. 4-1 *The checks in this detail of an oak sculpture have been filled with beeswax.*

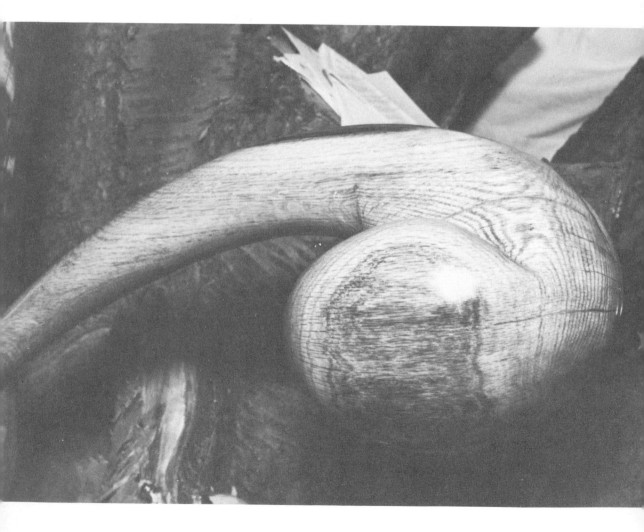

the check, the wood will not absorb the stain or coat of finish. Allow the filler to set for 15 or 20 minutes, then sand with a fine sandpaper until it is flush with the wood surface and removed from the surrounding area. Plastic Wood thinner is available if the filler becomes too hard to work with.

The major disadvantage of wood-putty fillers is that they dry hard and are not responsive to changes in the wood from heat, cold, or humidity. If you must fill a deep crevice in a large piece, try a pliable putty or a petroleum-based filler, available at craft-supply and hardware stores under various brand names. These will prevent the entire piece from splitting under different atmospheric conditions.

Stains

Staining highlights the color of the wood or intensifies an otherwise unnoticeable grain. It also can be used to imitate the tone and color of another type of wood. Pine, oak, and other light woods are often stained to bring out hidden grain patterns. Some woods with a nearly indistinguishable grain become beautifully exotic with the right stain or with a combination of stains.

Before applying a stain, you must sand the piece thoroughly, wet it to raise the grain, and sand again after it dries.

Water-Base Stains

Water-base stains come in powdered form and are reconstituted by dissolving the powder in near-boiling water. The dyes, called aniline dyes, deeply penetrate the wood and color it much the way that fabric dyes color cloth. The major advantage of water-base stains is the large variety of shades that can be obtained. Blending two or more colors can make just about any shade.

Stains vary in color intensity from one manufacturer to another, even though they are called by the same wood name. To find the stain intensity for your carving, experiment on a scrap of the same stock and test the different colors of stains in small sections. Another advantage of water-base stain is that it remains clear on the wood and will not cloud the surface or muddy the grain. The final factor is the cost: water-base stains are inexpensive.

Water-base stains have several drawbacks. Because water raises the grain of the wood, any piece to be stained must first be thoroughly dampened (not dripping wet), dried overnight, then sanded smooth. Once a piece has been stained, however, there is a risk of an unevenly stained finish. And water-base stains will streak if they are not applied carefully. Applying two thin coats of light stain, rather than one thick coat, will give you more control over the depth of color. Remember that the rough spots on unevenly sanded and tool-marked pieces will absorb more stain, so sand thoroughly before applying stain.

Here are a few rules to follow for the best results:

1. Apply the stain with a thoroughly wet but not dripping brush. If the brush starts to dry out, the strokes will not blend evenly.
2. Always brush along with grain. Crossing the grain may force more stain into the wood pores and leave darker spots.
3. Always allow the stain to dry for 4 to 6 hours before applying another coat.

Penetrating-oil stains are popular because the oil penetrates deeply and leaves the grain clear with an overall transparent quality. Penetrating oils are purchased ready to use, so there is the added advantage of convenience. The one major drawback, however, is that one stain will not give the same color to all types of wood. For example, red maple stain will intensify the red tones of a piece of red maple but will give an orangish cast to oak or pine. The appropriate color can be obtained only on the type of wood the stain was made for. Test the stain first on a scrap of the same stock as the piece itself.

Penetrating-Oil Stains

Oil stains often bleed through other finishes and change color. This can be prevented by sealing the surface with a thin coat of shellac and allowing it to dry thoroughly. Shellac can be thinned with denatured alcohol: 1 part shellac to 2 parts alcohol.

Penetrating-oil stains are readily absorbed by open-grain and soft woods. Because the color penetrates, more time should be allowed before wiping off the excess. Ordinarily, the exposed end grain will darken significantly from overabsorption of the stain, but you can minimize darkening by sealing the ends with a thin coat of shellac or linseed oil before applying the stain. Always allow coats of thinned shellac or oils to dry thoroughly before applying penetrating-oil stain to the entire piece. Oil-base stains do not raise the grain as do water-base ones. However, for a smooth, blemish-free finish, sand the fuzzy grain before staining.

Some pointers in applying penetrating-oil stain:

1. Sand the piece thoroughly. Rough or unevenly

sanded areas will become darker when the stain is applied.

2. Because penetrating oil is designed to penetrate, make sure the piece is clean. Any dirt, dust, or oil marks will prevent proper absorption and the piece will be splotchy.

3. Use a wet but not dripping brush. Choose a size that is appropriate to the size of the carving. Keeping the brush and the piece wet will prevent dark marks from the overlapping brush strokes.

4. Always work in the direction of the grain. Crossing the grain will cause streaks.

5. After applying the stain, wipe off the excess with a clean rag. (These rags can be highly combustible and should be washed or disposed of immediately.)

6. Allow the piece to dry for 24 hours before topcoating it. Oil-base stain dries much slower than water- or alcohol-base stains.

Alcohol-Base Stains

Mixing alcohol-base stain is similar to mixing water-base stains. The more dye dissolved in the alcohol, the deeper the stain. A difference to note, however, is that not all dyes are both water- and alcohol-soluble. Read each container carefully.

Alcohol stains will not raise the grain of the wood, but for the best results, follow the sanding-wetting-sanding procedure before applying. The transparency of the mixture leaves a beautifully clear surface with no muddying or clouding of the grain. The same factor that makes this stain a plus is also the major disadvantage. Alcohol dries rapidly, so unless the piece is stained quickly and evenly, streaks and overlapping marks will occur. On a small piece, however, it is often possible to coat it with one brushful, thus eliminating any marks.

To apply alcohol-base stain:

1. Prepare the surface by sanding and cleaning it thoroughly.
2. Brush on the stain in the direction of the grain and work at a good pace to prevent streaking, keeping in mind the alcohol's rapid drying time.
3. Apply additional coats when the stain is no longer tacky to the touch.

The color of the stain will deepen considerably when a second coat is applied.

Wax Stains

Wax stains, composed of wax and an oil-penetrating stain, are easy to apply, give a good, clear finish to the wood, and do not raise the grain. Because of the oil penetration, the stain becomes part of the wood. As with all penetrating oils, the colors work well only on the type of wood the stain was intended for. Walnut stain, for example, will not give a very pleasing tone to pine or maple, but it will make a piece of walnut glow.

To apply wax stains:

1. Sand the piece smooth, and make sure that it is free of dust and dirt.
2. Apply the wax with a cloth, which gives more control than a brush. After 5 or 10 minutes, wipe off the remaining stain with a clean cloth.
3. Allow the stain to dry for approximately 24 hours.

Wax seals the pores of the wood and protects the carving against dust and dirt, but it is not moisture-resistant. Hand-buffing with a paste wax will impart a satiny finish and protect the wood.

Varnish Stains

Varnish stains are varnishes that have a penetrating stain mixed in. While you can stain and finish in only one step, the end result is usually not worth the time saved. These stains tend to muddy the grain, and they are difficult to apply evenly without streaking. In general, these stains are inferior for woodcarvings.

Clear Finishes

Clear finishes have a dual purpose: to enhance either the natural grain of the wood or the stained surface, and to protect the surface from dirt, dust, and moisture. Many commercial finishes are mainly intended for furniture or wood floors, so any one will offer more than adequate protection for woodcarvings.

After staining, and before the final protective coat is applied, wipe all dust from the wood with a tack rag.

Wax

Commercial paste or liquid waxes impart a beautiful, protective sheen to wood. Most paste waxes contain some proportion of carnauba wax, one of the hardest waxes available and the major ingredient in floor waxes. Another popular type of wax finish is beeswax mixed with turpentine. The mixture is rubbed over the entire piece with cheesecloth. After allowing it to set for just a few minutes, buff the surface to a clear gloss.

Paste floor wax and good wax-based shoe polishes can be used successfully on some pieces to darken

Fig. 4-2 *The black walnut dachs-hund in Chapter 5 was finished with neutral wax shoe polish and buffed to a high gloss.*

Fig. 4-3 *The small basswood dachshund in Chapter 5 was finished with neutral wax shoe polish and buffed to a satiny sheen.*

the surface and enhance the wood. These are perhaps the easiest waxes to apply. The wax is rubbed into a soft cloth and worked evenly onto the surface (the same as the carnauba/paraffin wax combinations). Allow the wax to set into the wood for a few minutes, then rub until glossy.

Boiled linseed oil mixed with a few drops of tur- *Oil* pentine is one of the more classic finishes. It applies easily, is readily absorbed, and polishes well. All traces of oil must be wiped off, however, or the surface will stay tacky for a long time, and will dry with a blotchy sheen. This process should be repeated several times the first day to ensure that the surface becomes adequately soaked. Always check the can of linseed oil to see if it has been preboiled.

Linseed oil tends to change slightly the color of some lighter woods. It will yellow the pale tones of white pine and deepen the browns of mahogany and black walnut. But it is a finish in itself. No topcoats of shellac or varnish are necessary.

Professional woodcarvers and furniture finishers often finish their pieces with tung oil (available commercially) because it offers a durable finish. A small amount of the oil is poured into the palm to warm it for faster penetration. The carving is then rubbed by hand with the oil, allowed to sit for a few moments, and then rubbed dry with a clean, soft cloth. This finish also allows for eash touch-ups if the piece becomes scratched or dry.

The standard rule for polishing oiled pieces is: once a day for a week; once a week for a month; once a month for a year; then once a year for the rest of your life. When the wood looks as if it is drying, a coat of oil will even the sheen right out. Small scratches can be covered with a cloth dipped in the oil and thinly smoothed on.

Penetrating Resin

Penetrating resin may be the simplest and most durable of the clear finishes. Penetrating finishes resist almost any type of damage, including that from water, chemicals, heat, and scratching, because they sink into the wood and dry within the structure of the pores. This action gives the wood a plasticlike hardness without the plastic look or feel.

Penetrating resins leave the grain clearer and more vivid than oils, varnishes, shellacs, or waxes. Available commercially under various brand names, they come as ready-to-apply liquids. One of their major advantages is the ease of application on detailed pieces.

If a penetrating-oil *stain* has been used, the resin finish will not change the color of the piece significantly. Water-base stains, when finished with the penetrating-resin as a top coating, *will* darken. Test on a piece of scrap stock before applying.

Some hints for applying penetrating resins:

1. Fill a brush or cloth with the resin and apply freely to the sanded and cleaned surface. Flow on a thick application. Hold the carving over a pan to catch the drippings.
2. An alternative method of application is to pour a small amount of resin into your hand and spread it over the wood. Use your fingers to get into the crevices.
3. Apply the resin frequently for about an hour to keep the surface wet. When dull spots appear, apply more resin.

Fig. 4-4 *The pine swan in Chapter 5 was finished with a clear penetrating resin to highlight the grain.*

4. Penetration is the key to this finish, so no liquid should be allowed to dry on the surface. After an hour of saturation, wipe off the excess resin. When the piece has set for a half hour, some of the resin will puddle on the surface. Wipe the wood again to prevent an uneven sheen after the finish dries.

5. Apply another coat after the previous coat has been allowed to dry for about 3 hours to ensure even penetration.

6. After a 24-hour interval and two or three applications, some of the resin will have surfaced and dried. Remove these blotchy, shiny spots with extra-fine steel wool moistened with a small amount of the liquid resin.

The beauty of this finish comes from its being in the wood, rather than on it. The grain remains clear and the color vivid.

Varnishes

Many varieties of varnish are available for both woodcarvers and furniture finishers. Oil-based varnishes such as tung oil and linseed oil dry much slower than synthetic resin and urethane varnishes, which can be a major disadvantage when working with large pieces. The longer the surface remains wet, the more opportunity for dust and dirt to settle onto the surface. Although hand rubbing can remove some minor dust particles and imperfections on the surface, it is difficult to remove much more than that and still have an even finish and high luster. Stains tend to darken under varnish, so test on scrap stock beforehand.

Synthetic varnishes dry faster, crack less, and look less like a plastic coating than oil-based ones.

Some guidelines for applying synthetic varnishes:

1. Make sure the piece is free of dust and dirt. Also make sure that the stain is dry. Wet stain will mix with the varnish and muddy the grain.
2. Thin the first coat of varnish with 1 part turpentine to 4 parts varnish.
3. Brush the varnish in the direction of the grain. Light plays an important role here because the proper amount of varnish must be applied if it is to self-level on the surface. Too little and there are thin spots, too much and it will puddle, take extremely long to dry, and possibly crack. Watch the surface of the wood against the light as the varnish flows out. This will allow you to correct any faults before the varnish dries.
4. Because varnishes remain tacky for a relatively long time, dust can be a major problem. A satiny gloss can be obtained with a little rubbing, which will eliminate a small amount of dust and dirt. This is the finish most woodcarvers and furniture finishers prefer. If a piece is small enough, after it is varnished a large box can be inverted over it to help cut down on the amount of particles that can reach the wet surface.
5. Each coat of varnish should be allowed to dry for 24 hours. Gently sand with a fine paper between coats to remove dust and brush marks. Wipe the surface with a tack rag before applying the next coat. Three coats of varnish are considered to be the minimum for best results.

After the final coat of varnish is completely dry, the surface can be rubbed to produce an even, satiny sheen. Depending on whether you want a flat or glossy surface, use either rubbing compound, steel wool, or sandpaper.

Rubbing Compound

A rubbing compound consists of an abrasive, such as pumice, in a lubricant. Felt makes an excellent rubbing pad, or you can simply apply the compound with your hand. Water or mineral oil can be used as the lubricant. Oil, however, tends to slow down the abrasiveness of the pumice. The results obtained with water and oil are nearly the same.

Mix the pumice with a sufficient amount of mineral oil to make a paste. Apply the paste liberally, rubbing with the grain until a satiny sheen is obtained. Rubbing compound is not recommended for detailed pieces because it can build up in the crevices and be difficult to remove.

The pumice mixture dries rapidly on the surface and needs to be softened with a damp sponge to prevent scratching the newly polished finish. Rub off the excess water deposited from the sponge with a soft chamois or with any soft, clean cloth. If a surface has been previously rubbed with oil and pumice, be sure to remove all traces of residue before applying a wax finish. Tung oil will work well for this. Then apply wax over the thoroughly cleaned surface for a rich gloss.

Steel Wool Method

Steel wool, used either dry or soaked in mineral oil, is one of the simplest mediums for rubbing. Use it mainly for smaller carvings to smooth recessed detail and hard-to-reach areas. For a satiny surface, never use steel wool that is coarser than grade 2/0 or 3/0.

Roll the steel wool into a ball and press onto the wood with the palm of your hand. Unfortunately, steel wool sheds little steel splinters that can become embedded in your fingers if you are not careful. To prevent this, you can wear rubber gloves. Apply even, medium pressure in the direction of the grain. Too much pressure or too much rubbing will abrade the surface.

In a good light, check for dust, dirt, and brush marks. Wipe away any steel-wool particles with a soft cloth. Such particles can scratch, so brush gently. When the surface is clear of blemishes and has the desired sheen, it is ready to be oiled or waxed.

An alternative method of steel-wooling is to soak the pad with a light mineral oil and rub as with dry steel wool. Wipe the finished surface with a soft cloth to remove any steel-wool particles.

Sandpaper and Oil

When you want a flat, dull surface with no sheen, you can sand the piece with oil and sandpaper. A 5/0 garnet paper is recommended for most hard finishes. Soak the paper in mineral oil, and using only moderate pressure, sand gently in the direction of the grain. Check the finish frequently in a good light. Wipe off the sanding residue with a clean, soft cloth. Always wipe in the direction of the grain; otherwise, the remaining grit may mar the finish.

Polishes

Recipes for Oil and Wax Polishes

If a smoother, glossier finish is desired after rubbing, clean and polish the surface with one of the following classic formulas. Always melt oils and waxes in a double-boiler. This is a highly combustible mixture, and direct heat can cause the liquid to boil over or splash and ignite.

Oil Polish 1:   1 pint raw linseed oil
1 pint turpentine
1 ounce beeswax

Heat the oil by placing it in a quart can in a larger can of hot water, or use a double-boiler. Break the wax into the oil. Remove the can of wax from the hot water when it has completely dissolved. Allow the solution to cool slightly, then add the turpentine. Blend the mixture well with a wooden spoon or spatula. When the mixture is completely cool, pour some onto a clean, soft rag and rub it evenly onto the piece. Polish to a high luster.

Oil Polish 2: $\frac{1}{2}$ pint acetic acid (vinegar)
$\frac{1}{2}$ pint paraffin oil
$\frac{1}{2}$ pint denatured alcohol

Mix the three ingredients well, then soak a soft cloth in the mixture. Apply freely to the surface, let the polish sit for a short while, then buff to a rich glow. If the mixture does not stay blended, stir it again. Never shake the mixture, since tiny bubbles will form that can dry on the finish and leave craters.

Wax Polish 1:   1 pound carnauba wax
1 pound paraffin wax
1 pint turpentine

Because carnauba wax is so hard, it cannot be used alone. Break it and the paraffin wax into small pieces and melt the two together in a double-boiler. When the waxes are completely melted, remove the mixture from the heat, cool slightly, and slowly add the turpentine. Stir constantly with a wooden spoon or spatula while adding the turpentine to blend the mixture well. When it has completely cooled, the mixture may be applied to the wood and buffed like any commercial paste wax. If the wax begins to solidify, reheat it carefully and slowly add more turpentine.

Wax Polish 2:   1 pound beeswax (white or brown)
$\frac{1}{2}$ pint turpentine

Cut the beeswax into shavings and add to the turpentine, which will dissolve it. To speed up the process, you can melt the wax first, allow it to cool slightly, and then add the turpentine. Note that if beeswax is not polished thoroughly, it will tend to streak.

For an exceptionally glossy, smooth surface, rottenstone and oil give results that are unsurpassed by any other polishing technique. Rottenstone is a fine abrasive powder derived from slate. It looks and feels like talcum powder, but when mixed with oil and rubbed over a finish, it produces a high gloss from its gentle abrasion. This type of finish requires a lot of work and is relatively expensive compared to other methods. However, the results on the right piece are beyond compare.

Make a rottenstone/oil paste of a good spreading consistency. If it is too thick, it will be difficult to work with. Apply the paste with your hand.

Rottenstone/Oil Polish

Rottenstone makes an excellent polish follow-up to a piece that has been rubbed with pumice and oil. After cleaning off the pumice/oil residue (tung oil is excellent for this), rub on the mixture immediately. Clean off the residue with a clean cloth, wiping in the direction of the grain. Use a little oil by itself if the rottenstone has started to cake on the surface. It should be softened to be removed; otherwise, minute scratches will mar the gloss.

French (Shellac) Polishing

French polishing is considered by many wood-carvers and furniture finishers to be the definitive finish for wood surfaces because it leaves the wood extremely smooth with a high luster. It consists of several coats of shellac and linseed oil, applied alternately, and a lot of rubbing. Nearly the same luster can be had for less work with the rottenstone/oil polish.

Shellacing is easier than varnishing, mainly because of the quicker drying time. Shellac dries dust-free, usually within a half hour. It flows on easily, adheres well, and waxes to a fine luster.

All of the finishes discussed in this chapter are available at most craft-supply and hardware stores (or see List of Suppliers). Trial and error with the many types of finish will lead you to your favorite. There is no right way to finish a woodcarving. These guidelines are useful mainly to prevent damaging the carving and to save you time.

CHAPTER 5
Six Woodcarving Projects

WOODCARVING is an ambiguous term that can cover a multitude of types of carvings. The six projects in this chapter fall into categories: chip carving, incised carving, high- and low-relief carving, intaglio, and carving in-the-round (described in Chapter 3). Each piece is actually a combination of carving methods, and artistic freedom is what makes each piece of carved art unique. Experimenting with the various carving methods and techniques will lead you to those that will complement your unique interests and abilities.

The projects and the step-by-step directions for carving, sanding, and finishing them are intended as a guide, but they are by no means the only way. They will give you experience with the various knives and carving tools and with the different methods of shaping the wood.

Whittling: Basswood Dachshund

A good first project for whittling in-the-round, which actually serves a dual purpose, is the basswood dachshund. The basswood is soft, with a fine grain that resists splitting, and it takes detail well.

It also can be finished in a variety of ways to produce a satisfying first attempt at whittling.

The small basswood dachshund, about 4" high, is an art work in itself, but it can also be used as a maquette (model) for the larger dachshund in black walnut in this chapter. Maquettes provide a visual reference for reproducing the image and keeping proportions accurate. Many artists use wax or clay instead of wood for the maquette. The type of material used for the models largely depends on the degree of durability you want. If you want a permanent art piece, of course use a more permanent medium.

Carving the Blank

Choose a rectangular block of wood and trace a rough outline of the begging dachshund. Any soft wood could be used. Fill as much of the blank as possible so that you won't waste too much wood. Try to design the piece to suit the shape as well as the type and color of the wood. For a small piece such as this, you can use a coping saw to remove the extraneous wood. If you are making a large piece, you would use a bandsaw. Sawing away the extraneous wood produces the rough outline, which is called a blank. From this blank, the finished art work emerges.

The first cuts should be made *with* the grain. Here the grain should run vertically because it will be easier to carve, and it will enhance the design. Carving against the grain makes the work just that—work. The wood will become chipped and gouged. This will detract from the finished piece if you have used a softer wood.

Start with a razor-sharp sheepfoot or spey-tip blade and pull the knife shallowly over the long lines of

Fig. 5-1 *Sculptor Clark Mester's maquettes.*

the dog's back (Fig. 5-4). Take care not to angle the blade too deeply or the wood will split and chip. The tool in Figure 5-5 is a spey-tip draw knife. The angled handle may seem cumbersome at times, but once you get used to it, you will find it easy to grip and hold. Until it is comfortable in your hand, you could use a thinner, narrower knife blade and make shallow, light cuts. Thicker blades can be forced too deeply at first. The lighter blade naturally feels more delicate, and you will automatically use less force.

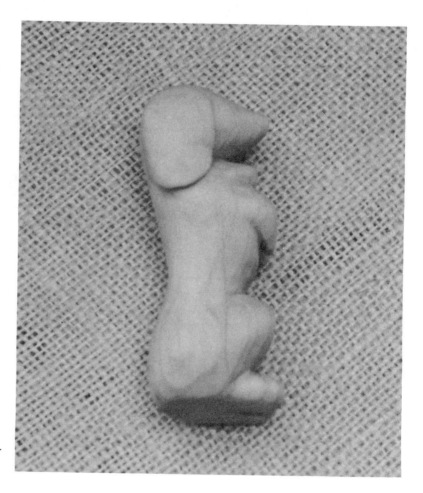

Fig. 5-2 *The dachshund, our first project.*

Fig. 5-3 *Basswood blank, roughed out.*

Fig. 5-4 *With a sheepfoot blade, make vertical cuts with the grain along the dachshund's back.*

Fig. 5-5 *Carving
with a spey-tip
draw knife.*

After working down one side of the dog's back,
turn the blank around and shave down the other side.
Turning and working all sides evenly will help keep
the dog's body in proper proportion. As the sides
begin to take shape, move downward and shape the
rump area and the feet (Fig. 5-6). How much wood
you remove and how you shape the hind legs and
feet are up to you.

Many beginning woodcarvers tend to shape too
lightly and remove too little wood from the blank.
The results are usually a squarish, unfinished looking piece. Removing a small amount at a time is an
excellent, safe technique, but continue to remove
small pieces slowly until the blank is rounded and
truly three-dimensional. Unless a squared-off look

Fig. 5-6 *Removing wood from the feet and rump area with the sheepfoot blade.*

is a specific of your design, rounding usually adds grace to the work.

As the back, rump, and feet begin to take shape, move upward to the front paws, shoulders, face, and ears (Figs. 5-7, 5-8, and 5-9). Outlining the paws and the ears first with a sharp tip makes it easier to remove just the proper depth from the face area. An elongated spear point is used in Figure 5-8. Making a stop cut around the ears with the tip of the knife helps prevent you from going beyond the boundaries (Fig. 5-10).

Remove the edge of the ear where it meets the face by making an incised, angled cut (not too deeply), and then cut at the same angle from the opposite side. Remove this chip with the tip of the blade. Be

Fig. 5-7 *Carving the area around the front paws.*

Fig. 5-8 *Trimming the shoulders and neck area with a slant-tip blade.*

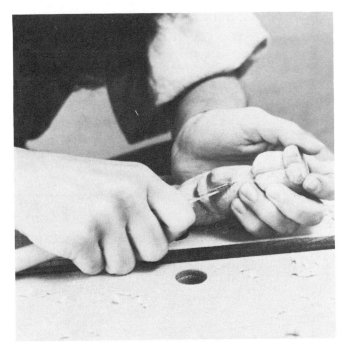

Fig. 5-9 *Carving the front paws and hind legs with the sheep-foot blade.*

Fig. 5-10 *Making a stop cut around the ears using a clip blade.*

very careful to prod the chip out gently. Don't pick at it forcefully. Making repeated cuts at the angle will give you the best results.

Hold the dog in the palm of your hand with the nose pointing away from you and note the vertical grain. Because this area is to be thinned significantly, cut with a slow sweeping gesture across the grain (Fig. 5-11). Many shallow cuts instead of large chipping cuts help keep the grain lines clear and the surface of the face smooth and crisp. Work from the top of the muzzle and gently curve the cuts around to the underside of the nose. Care and time taken on this portion will help eliminate a lot of effort later when you sand and finish the piece. If you are careless, the surface will be gouged and crushed.

Fig. 5-11
Smoothing the muzzle and neck.

Before removing more wood from under the ears, be sure that your blade is razor sharp. The dachshund's ears should be thin and appear to hang away from the head. The vertical grain helps to strengthen the thin ear lines, but be careful to remove only small pieces at a time. This can be done in the same way as the pieces were removed around the face and the ear. If you angle the blade from each side, taking care to keep the cuts shallow, you will achieve the correct depth and thinness.

If at any point the blade becomes lodged in the wood, gently rock it back and forth until it works free. If it does not release easily even when rocked, use another sharp blade to cut it out. Pulling too roughly or trying to hit it out with another tool can damage the wood and the tools.

When the body is roughed out to the proportions you visualized at the start, it is time to start carving more detail and finishing touches to make the dog more realistic, even though it is still greatly stylized, as in the spaces between the paws and hind legs. Removing these portions of wood will give a greater illusion of lightness, which is what you want if the dog is to look even and balanced.

Use a slant-tipped blade to cut into the deeper recesses under the nose above the collarbone. This maneuver entails cutting across the grain, so use an extremely sharp knife edge. If the blade is not sufficiently sharpened, it will crush the grain. This cut-off portion of the end of the grain is called the end grain. When the piece is finished, it will absorb more of the stain or finish and consequently be darker than the rest of the piece. This darkening tends to illuminate any errors in your carving techniques, and it can ruin an otherwise well-carved piece. As with the areas around the nose and ears, gentle, shallow cuts are preferable to deeper, forceful cuts.

To give the dachshund body more definition, trim the stomach area quite thinly for the characteristic "hotdog" look. Using a sharp sheepfoot blade, gradually whittle down the sides and then the front. Shaving off shallow slices leaves the surface smooth and blemish-free. If you gouge the wood, simply whittle the stomach a little leaner, then sand out the remaining marks. Of course, removing an error works only up to a certain point—then the problem becomes part of the piece. It's easier to work carefully and avoid mistakes than it is to fix them.

One area that will need a great deal of wood removed is around the paws. To prevent the finished dog from looking too squared-off, curve the sides and then the paws slightly inward at the toes. This better defines the legs from the sides and the stomach. The collarbone should be smooth and show no ridge where it meets the front paws. After curving a small amount of the wood around the collarbone slightly upward, sand it to finish shaping it.

Once the dog is completed to your satisfaction, examine it carefully from all directions to be certain it is in proportion and sufficiently carved "in-the-round." If not, this is the last opportunity to correct major flaws with a knife. Viewing the piece with this in mind allows you to fix any rough spots now.

The blank used for this dachshund had one particularly rough side. Trying to remove this extra roughness by sanding could be tedious and frustrating. Shaving with a sharp blade will smooth the roughness more quickly. This roughness was still visible after most of the major cuts had been made. Care was taken not to slice too deeply and mar the lines of the dog. Sanding will remove small errors and smooth the tool marks, but it will not fix mistakes of any size. Finishing smoothes only the surface, not the shape and design of the carving.

Because basswood is a relatively soft wood that tends to fuzz when sanded, several steps are necessary to prepare the surface before finishing. For the first sanding, use a moderately coarse grade of paper. For basswood, 120-grit aluminum-oxide sandpaper would be best. If you are using another type of wood, experiment with a medium-grit sandpaper in an unobtrusive place on the piece. If the wood abrades too rapidly, the grade is too coarse. Adjust the grade of sandpaper until you achieve the best results. Continue sanding until the piece is smooth.

Sanding

Rough areas that are difficult to reach with a piece of sandpaper can be sanded with a nail file or emery board (Fig. 5-13). The rougher side is excellent for the first sanding and the finer side is perfect for finishing. Small rifflers can be used to smooth hard-to-reach areas. Either a pointed-tip riffler or an oval-shaped tip will reach into the recesses and remove the excess waste as well as smooth the wood. These tools are highly abrasive, so use very little pressure.

Before doing the finer, finishing sanding, dampen the piece with water and allow it to dry. Wetting the surface causes the fine grain lines to raise. To dampen, wipe the surface with a wet but wrung-out cloth. Never immerse the piece in water or dowse it under the faucet. When the wood is dry, sand it smooth with 220-grit paper. Always use a light hand when

Fig. 5-12 *The roughly carved dog is ready to be sanded.*

Fig. 5-13 *Filing rough, hard-to-reach areas with an emery board.*

sanding. Too much sanding after wetting and drying will remove this raised grain and cause more fuzz. Then the process will have to be repeated, and with poorer results. Sanding in the direction of the grain with the 220-grit paper leaves the surface smooth and well prepared for whatever type of finish you choose.

Before selecting a finish, decide how you want it to look. This dog has uncluttered lines and subtle grain patterns that won't interfere with the design. To keep the natural light color of the wood, transparent wax shoe polish was rubbed into the wood and alternately buffed and layered with a soft piece of old terry-cloth toweling. Each time polish was applied, the crack (check) on the right side was filled

Finishing

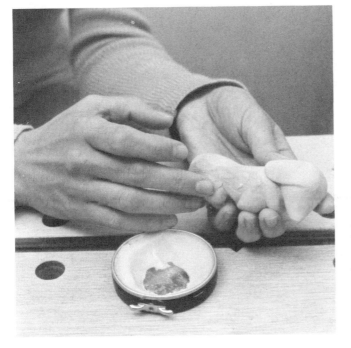

Fig. 5-14 *Neutral wax shoe polish is hand-rubbed onto the sanded dog. The walnut base is finished with the same polish.*

with as much wax as it would take. Because it is so porous, the end grain will absorb much more wax than will the sides.

Any area of the dog that is cut diagonally or perpendicular to the direction of the grain is end grain. Therefore, the tops of the collarbone, paws, and hind legs, and feet will take more wax. Apply several sparse applications to the end grain and observe how much the wax stains or darkens this area before proceeding with each successive waxing.

Buffing is the real key to a clear, even appearance. And *uniform* buffing is what you should strive for. Make sure that some areas are not shinier than others. It is easier to apply additional coats of wax than it is to try to buff off caked wax, so go slowly, remembering that many light applications are necessary before the wood pores become saturated and the piece uniformly shiny.

The Base

A base is not a necessary part of a carving, but when a piece is as light in color and small in size like this dachshund, it is shown off to its best advantage by a base of a contrasting color. The base in Figure 5-15 was made from a scrap piece of black walnut about 1¾" high. A router was used to form the outer edge, but it can easily be ornamentally hand-carved or even left square.

The flat, horizontal lines of the base accent the slender vertical lines of the dog. The base also gives the dog more stability as a display piece. The walnut was sanded with 120-grit paper and finished with 220 grit. It was sealed with the same transparent wax shoe polish used on the basswood dog and then buffed to a softer shine. The base should never compete

Fig. 5-15 *The finished dachshund mounted on the walnut base.*

with the carving, so the shine was toned down by not using as many coats of wax and not buffing to a high gloss. If the last thin coat is smoothed but not buffed, it will produce a dull gloss.

The dachshund is now ready for display or to be used as a model for the larger, more difficult dachshund in walnut.

Carving in-the-Round: Black Walnut Dachshund

Black walnut was chosen for this larger dachshund because it is an oily wood that carves easily and finishes beautifully. The grain runs lengthwise to complement the long, thin lines of the dog's body. Because walnut is a hard wood and it is sturdy enough not to split at the thin points, the thinness of the piece is not a concern. The design of this dog is more simplified than the basswood one in order to heighten the grain pattern and to allow the wood to shine without distracting details. This dachshund is about 18″ high, and it can be carved from any hard wood.

Carving the Blank

After selecting the wood, rough-cut the design. Many woodcarvers sketch their pattern onto the wood in pencil to make it easier to keep proportion when using either a bandsaw or coping saw for bosting (Fig. 5-16). When you are ready to begin carving, secure the piece to the work surface so that it won't move around while being struck. Choose a clamp or vise that suits the size and shape of the wood. Figure 5-17 shows the vertical vise of the Black and Decker Work-Mate, which will hold the piece sufficiently while hand-holding the carving tools or striking them with a mallet. The piece should be worked evenly all over.

Fig. 5-16 *Using a bandsaw to cut the rough shape of the dachshund. Because walnut is such a hard wood, this step saves time and frustration.*

Fig. 5-17 *Cutting across the grain with a ½" straight gouge.*

The head of the dachshund will be much thinner than the body, and the ears will be wider. Begin by cutting inward from the nose (Fig. 5-17). Cutting across the grain, make shallow cuts with the $\frac{1}{2}''$ straight gouge. This tool is excellent for these basic big cuts. The control afforded by the slight curvature of the blade helps prevent gouging and overcutting the wood. Moving down from the pointed nose, remove the wood from between the paws and legs will keep the carving balanced (Fig. 5-18).

Turn the piece sideways and line up the ears using the $\frac{5}{16}''$ V-tool. After doing the ear (do only one side at a time to save having to clamp and unclamp the piece), and move down to the body (Figs. 5-19 A, B, and C). A great deal of wood must be removed from the thin midsection of the dog. The $\frac{3}{8}''$ straight gouge is recommended for these cuts. Shape one side roughly, then turn the piece over and do the other side. This is a good time to check the sculpture to see if any areas are unbalanced.

Reclamp the piece and start again with the nose, working to the neck, and remove a small amount at a time (Fig. 5-20). The $\frac{1}{4}''$ skew chisel will make the deeper slices between the paws, legs, and feet. Because the lines of the design and the lines of the dog run with the grain, work at a slight angle to the grain to prevent splitting the wood. When a pattern calls for cutting across the grain (as with the nose), use a very sharp blade and make short, slow strokes.

Working on the back of the dog, carefully remove the wood from the back of the head between the ears (Fig. 5-21). This area also runs with the grain, so be careful that the chips you remove are not too large. Aiming the chisel on the diagonal across the back

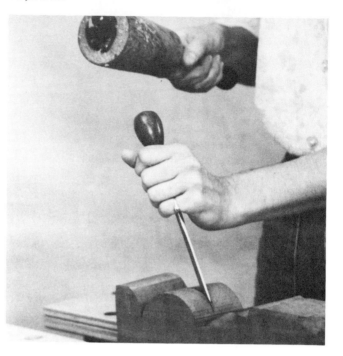

Fig. 5-18 *Separating the hind legs and feet. The same technique is used to separate the front paws.*

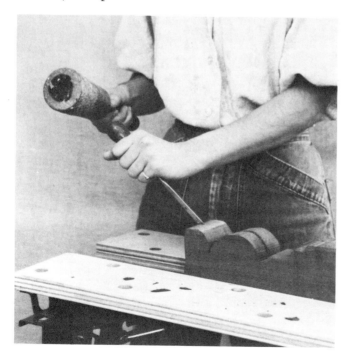

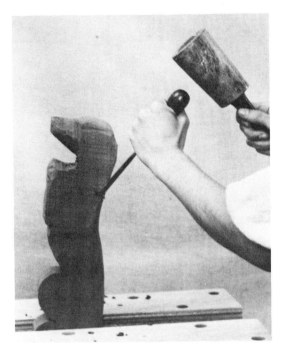

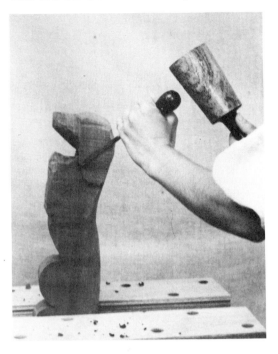

Fig. 5-19 *Outlining and defining the ear with a* $\frac{3}{8}''$ *straight gouge.*

Fig. 5-20 *Working downward to the collarbone and front paws.*

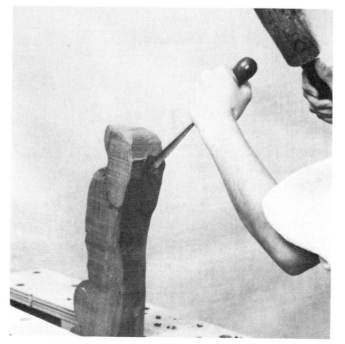

Fig. 5-21 *Carefully shaping the back of the head between the ears.*

of the head helps prevent gouging and splintering the wood.

Secure the piece front side up and smooth and round the back by removing the sharp corners on the sides (Fig. 5-22). This area can be carved last because there is not much more to do than smooth and curve the sides to balance the begging posture. The $\frac{3}{8}$" gouge works well for this area. The blade must be razor sharp because you must cut into the grain. Rotate the dog in the vise after cutting evenly down one side at a time to keep the proper balance and proportion.

The area between the nose and the collarbone should be carefully worked to prevent crushing and smashing the more delicate end grain. Besides the waist and stomach, this area needs to have the most wood removed to stay in proportion with the slender lines and the light appearance of the dog's body.

Because there is no real detail on this piece, all you have to do now is turn the dog and carve it on all sides with a $\frac{3}{8}$" or the $\frac{1}{2}$" straight gouge until it is long, slender, and well balanced.

Sanding

To obtain a highly polished, silky-smooth appearance, you must do a great deal of sanding. Because black walnut is so oily and dense a wood, use a coarse grit of sandpaper. Start with 80 or 100 grit. Sand in the direction of the grain to ease the marks on the wood that need to be removed during successive sandings with lighter grade papers.

After the coarse paper has removed the machine and tool marks, it is time to start the real smoothing process. Experiment with 120 grit to see if it is coarse enough to further the smoothing. This may be the

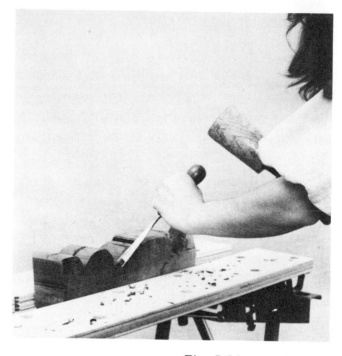

Fig. 5-22 *Continuing to thin the midsection.*

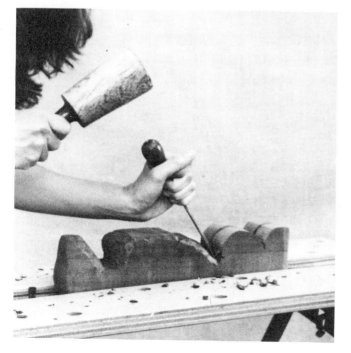

most tedious of the finishing tasks, but the effort is well worth it.

After the 120 paper has removed the finer mars on the piece, 220 will fine sand the dog to a satiny smoothness. At this stage the wood should be dampened to raise the grain and allowed to dry. When the wood is thoroughly dried, the 220 paper will remove this fuzz, leaving a satin-smooth surface ready for the desired finish.

Finishing

Several finishes would work well on this dachshund. One is a penetrating water-base finish. This finish is applied to the wood, allowed to soak in and then reapplied until the surface is saturated. The excess can be wiped off and the piece left to dry in a dust-free environment. Flow on the finish freely, and then smooth around the piece, making sure to get it deeply into the crevices. Applications may take a full hour to saturate the wood, and then need to be wiped off. Extra-fine steel wool will smooth any blotchy areas and reduce the gloss to a satiny finish.

Beeswax and turpentine is another good finish. Rub the piece with the beeswax and turpentine mixture, then buff to a clear gloss with a soft cloth. Because beeswax is soft, it tends to smear, so you must buff patiently.

Another finish, and the one that was used on this piece, is wax shoe polish. The transparent, neutral shades darken the wood slightly and enhance the natural grain. This is perhaps one of the simplest and yet durable methods of finishing. Apply the wax lightly, allow it to set for about a half hour to an hour, and then buff it to a high shine. The more buffing you do, the shinier the gloss will be. If you

Fig. 5-23 *The finished dachshund.*

want a dull gloss, apply a last coat of wax, let it dry, and then lightly polish the piece. Applying additional coats and rubbing vigorously will produce an even higher gloss.

Carving and Whittling: The Pine Swan

The swan is an excellent example of a contemporary sculpture that has graceful lines yet is quick and simple to carve. White pine was chosen because of its softness and its attractive grain figure and pattern when waxed. The swan, which is 16″ high, could be carved in any other wood.

Carving the Blank

A bandsaw or coping saw are of immeasurable help in saving time and effort at the beginning of this project. The coping saw removes the extraneous wood from the inside of the neck and forms a tighter arch for the finished piece. Starting with a large block of wood, draw the swan design on the wood. This guideline will soon disappear with carving. The important part is the inside of the curve. If it is kept even from the beginning, then the outside curve and the sloping neck line will remain even and balanced.

Either carving tools (mainly the $\frac{3}{8}$″ gouge) or whittling knives can be used to smooth the rough lines of the head and neck. The beak is thin and sloping, and care should be taken here not to cut the bill too narrow. This narrowness could throw off the balance and cause the wood to break at an awkward point.

After removing the larger portions of waste wood, the main consideration is to reduce the boxy look of the neck and body. This design does call for a certain squareness to the body to show off the wood and the swan shape.

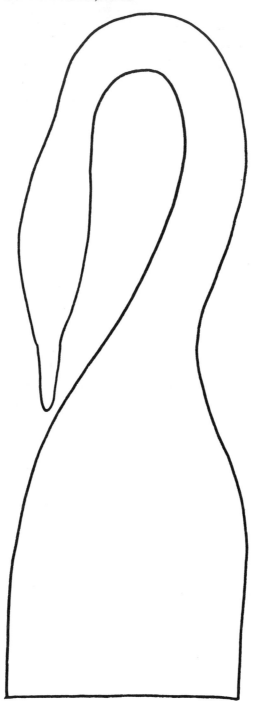

Fig. 5-24 *Pattern for the swan, side view.*

Slicing slowly with the razor-sharp blade, gently slope the neck lines down to the body. It is necessary to cut across the grain at certain points in the curve, but for the most part the cuts are straightforward.

The ease of this piece comes from the simplicity of design. As you carve, it is easy to see where and what should be carved or smoothed next. The idea here is to take off as little as possible and still define the swan shape.

The swan requires a great deal of heavy sanding. *Sanding* A very coarse (perhaps 100 grit) sandpaper can be used to smooth any gouges or nicks in the wood. Because the lines are so clean and simple, there can be no room for any surface blemishes or mars, which would destroy the symmetry.

After sanding the mars and nicks with the 100-grit paper, switch down one grade to a 120 grit and sand until the surface is evenly smooth.

The piece of pine used for the swan that is illustrated had an interesting circular grain configuration that was used to advantage around the eye of the swan when the design was planned. This area, as well as the strong vertical grain, needs to be sanded particularly well to have the pattern outshine any of the other attributes of the wood.

While sanding, pay particular attention to the inside of the neck. Dampen the piece to raise the grain and allow it to dry. Sand smooth with 220-grit paper.

The finish for this piece should be fairly high gloss *Finishing* or at least a satin gloss to catch the light and show off the lines and the wood. Because the grain was so evident in interesting places, the wood on this swan was left natural and a water-base penetrating finish

Fig. 5-25 *Note the grain configurations of the wood around the swan's eye.*

Fig. 5-26 *The finished swan.*

applied. The surface was coated liberally and re-coated at the first signs of dullness. After the finish was absorbed, the piece was set in a dust-free box to dry. Periodically, it was removed to wipe any pooled residue from the surface. After two or three hours, the piece was left alone to dry.

A paste of tung oil and rottenstone was used for the final buffing and polishing. This polishing removes any superficial marks and dust particles in the finish. It also gives the swan a high-gloss, mirrorlike finish. This piece would also be attractive stained in a dark cherry or walnut.

Texturing and Random Patterning: A Basswood Squirrel

The basswood squirrel looks as though it is an easier project than the two dachschunds and swan, but the actual carving process is more difficult. Random texturing requires a good eye and sharp tools. It also employs more techniques and different tools than the other projects.

The squirrel, which is 9″ high, is made of basswood because its indistinguishable grain pattern will not compete with the textured finish. Any close-grained wood could be used. The color can be left natural or stained to imitate a darker wood. Because basswood is so soft, it is usually not worked with carving tools and a mallet. This piece was done with both hand pressure and mallet pressure, and with knives and carving tools. The grain of basswood can be crushed if too much force is applied and if the tools are not razor sharp.

Carving and Texturing the Blank

As with the black walnut dachshund, do the rough outline of the squirrel with a bandsaw or coping saw, and then rough out the shape with chisels and gouges.

Alternatively, you can bost with a large, shallow chisel or gouge and a medium-weight mallet. Either way, be sure to keep the dimensions in proportion or the piece will become more and more lopsided as the project progresses. Random texturing tends to highlight any errors or rough spots rather than help disguise them. Even though the texturing appears to have been done haphazardly, the carving must be planned and well thought out along the way.

The final rough cuts were made with the sheepfoot draw knife and a spear-tip knife to reach the smaller, deeper areas. The space between the ears is a particularly difficult place to reach without damaging the soft grain and wood pores. Instead of spotlighting a smooth spot between the ears, rough the area with a slant-tipped skew chisel to match the rougher texture of the body (Fig. 5-27).

The basic steps for shaping the squirrel are the same as with the other projects. But keep in mind that the texturing process will remove a certain amount of wood. You must take this into consideration at the rough cutting and carving stage so that the squirrel does not become too thin. This project is more abstract in shape than the others, which means that you must rely on your imagination rather than following a prescribed form and details.

After making the rough cuts to define the stylized shape, do some small practice texturing cuts to determine the size and pattern as shown in Figure 5-28. Begin the rough shaping with the head and continue down to the legs and knees to keep the piece in proportion (Fig. 5-29). Turn the piece frequently and do even and overall carving so that you don't remove too much wood from one area and not enough from another.

Fig. 5-27 *Rough-ing the area be-tween the ears with a slant-tip skew chisel.*

Fig. 5-28 *Practice texturing cuts in the rough stage helps to define the squirrel's size and shape.*

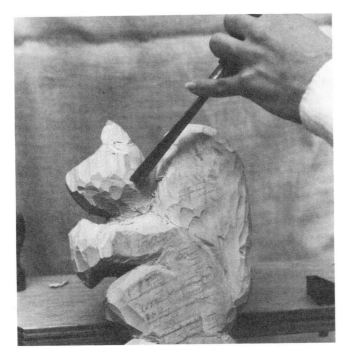

Fig. 5-29 *Practice texture cuts.*

Fig. 5-30 *Defining the area between the body and tail. Choose a gouge according to the depth of the groove you want. You can also use a V-tool.*

The feet present a unique problem. They either could be large and caricatured, or they could be shortened. However, shortening them increases the risk of splitting the thinner wood in this area. Because of the abstract nature of the form, the feet on this squirrel were shortened for a more stylized look by using a shallow gouge and light hand pressure to remove just the tips. A spear-tip knife was used to shape and texture them gently after they were shortened to the desired size. Shaping this more fragile area with a knife allows more control than a chisel or gouge and a mallet.

Whereas the walnut dachshund was designed on longer, thinner lines, requiring precautions to be taken with the more fragile areas that would chip or crack easily, the squirrel is just the opposite. The lines of the design are broader and flatter, and to keep the total effect true, the broader proportion must be carefully maintained.

After shaping the head, ears, knees, and tail, texturing them slightly just to get an idea of the effect, repeat the entire shaping process, starting at the head and ears and proceeding to the knees and tail.

One difficult area to shape is the point between the squirrel's tail and body. This line must be defined to distinguish it from the two sides, yet it must maintain texture. To do this efficiently, use a gouge, the size determined by the degree of depth of the groove you want (Fig. 5-30). This groove can also be made by slicing from one side to a midpoint and then cutting away the other side. This is similar to the technique used for carving the letters in the sign-plaque project.

The groove can be made quickly with a very sharp gouge or V-tool. When the groove seems to be the proper depth and width, use the same sized gouge to feather the wood slightly on either side. The same sized gouge keeps all the lines in proportion. Look at the piece from all angles to adjust the design.

Keep in mind that the particular flaws that occur during carving and texturing can be turned into assets and make the piece unique. For example, when the squirrel illustrated was rough-carved, the hands were much too large for the body and were ungainly in comparison with the rest of the features. Instead of removing more wood from this area, it was decided that the squirrel should be shown holding a nut. The nut does not need much more definition than the rest of the squirrel; it can simply be incorporated into the abstract design. The ends that were to have been fingers were tapered and rounded, and the top portion became the nut (Fig. 5-31). The broad hand area allows the head and knees also to be chunkier and therefore in proportion.

The inside of the ears is another tricky spot because it must have some depth, yet it is in a thinner, easily chipped area. A $\frac{1}{4}''$ gouge was used to carve out the interior of the ears in one motion (Fig. 5-32). The gouge was forced with the mallet to do the cut all in one motion to prevent splitting. This cut takes a firm yet gentle tap. The mallet should not be drawn back too far. If you make too many taps, the danger of splitting increases.

The cuts to the ears should be the same size as the cuts on the face. Don't worry about tool marks, although try to keep them to a minimum.

Fig. 5-31 *Fashioning the nut. Always keep in mind the possibility of splitting.*

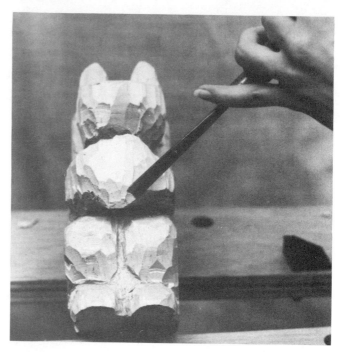

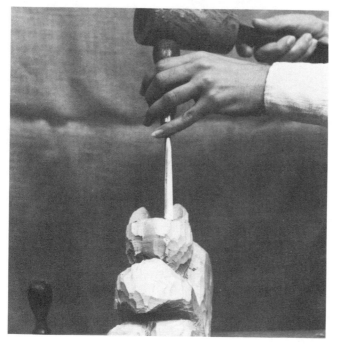

Fig. 5-32 *Mallet and gouge should be held lightly but firmly.*

Carve the entire front of the squirrel, turn it, and carve again until it is in proper proportion.

Because the finished squirrel will not be sanded, like the other projects, the deep cuts, flaws, and rough cuts will be evident unless textured out of the finish. The final texturing must be done slowly and in the same area before going on to another area. The blending of one space to another is very important to the finished appearance. Otherwise, the piece will have a patchy, unprofessional look.

The Final Texturing

Starting at the tail sides, carve one row with a gouge of an appropriate size for the entire area. If you use different sizes, the proportion will be thrown off. And if the grooves overwhelm the piece, it will turn into a study in surface texture without the form.

To begin texturing the tail, place the squirrel upright in the vise and make the cuts in a uniform depth around the outside edge (Fig. 5-33). Bring the gouge back to the starting point and recut the cuts until they are smooth and clean against the grain. After this initial carving, look at the piece from a distance to determine if the cuts should be deeper or wider. Now is the time to determine how much wood should be removed. The piece easily could be carved down to half its original size if you try to equalize the depth of too many uneven cuts. Also be careful not to make one area deeper than another, unless doing so helps to define some feature of the piece. This part of the texturing process is where patience is so important. The cuts that make abstract forms so unique and interesting are tedious and time-consuming.

The tail can be shaped as well as textured by these cuts. Just be certain that each cut is uniform and

Fig. 5-33 *Beginning the tail texturing. Again, work with the grain.*

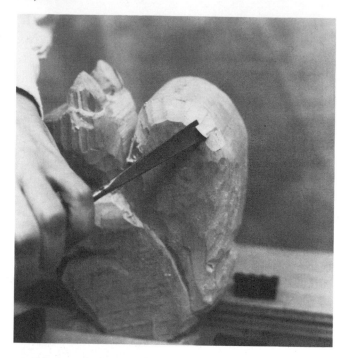

Fig. 5-34 *Defining the loose tail dip by gouging shallowly.*

follows the shape of the tail. Study each angle before striking. The one exception is the area where the tail dips in and then out again. This can be layered down to a narrower cut and then gradually widened to give the area more definition. To keep the cuts from showing too much tool marking, use a shallow gouge (perhaps a ⅝″ No. 5) to define the top area of the tail dip (Fig. 5-34). The tool marks can then be finished by carefully stop-cutting in the opposite direction with an angled skew chisel (Fig. 5-35). To prevent slipping and gouging the wood, angle the chisel slightly so that it is parallel with the wood surface. Any errors in this area will be glaring. The skew should be razor sharp to slice away gently the rough edges of the gouge marks. Make the upper cuts with the shallow gouge and tap the mallet gently but firmly to cut cleanly.

To maintain the best overall finished look, after each area has been sufficiently carved, go back to the area before it and blend any marks that are apparent. By turning the piece frequently, you can more easily maintain smooth lines and even cuts. To refine the front cuts and the inside cuts (around the legs and under the chin) before adding the finishing touches, retouch them with knife blades, not carving tools. The knives are easier to guide because they are smaller and fit into the hand better.

The major area, because it is the most visible, is the back of the tail. To texture it successfully, start the cuts at the top of the dip and gradually work up to the top of the tail (Fig. 5-36). Each set or row of cuts should slightly overlap the previous ones. The cuts in Figure 5-36 were angled in slightly, with each row becoming more angled until midway up the tail.

Then they were straightened. The effect here is that of a bushiness at the base and middle and a narrowing at the top. This suggests motion, like a nervous little form about to run, and causes the eye to follow the tail in different directions. The lines of the texturing are what create this effect in any project. Straight, uniform lines are more stable and stationary than erratic, although even, lines. This squirrel does not pretend to imitate reality. Instead, the random texturing suggests the motion of a small, quick animal that has paused for a moment.

Incised Carving: Pine Sign Plaque

The sign plaque project provides an easy way to accustom your hand to handling carving tools. Practice first with the different tools on a scrap piece of wood. Try to carve an initial into the wood to get a feel for what kind of control you will need when following a pattern. While handling the tools is relatively easy, guiding them with precise control takes more practice.

The name sign illustrated, made of pine, is intended for indoor use. The dimensions are 10″ by 12″. If you want to make an outside sign, such as for a front yard or for a family camper identification, use a more durable type of wood that can withstand the elements. Some woods, such as cedar, even weather with age and become more beautiful. The pinkish cedar ages to a silver-gray. Redwood would be another good choice because of its natural durability and its ability to withstand decay and insect penetration.

The size of the finished sign, the purpose it is intended for, and the design to be carved onto the

Fig. 5-35 *Finishing the tail dip with stop cuts made with an angled skew.*

Fig. 5-36 *Texturing the tail. Strive for a stylized effect of simulated fur.*

wood are decisions that must be made before start-ing. The design possibilities are limited only by the wood space and your imagination. Design your own letters, or use a monogram chart from a needlework book, selecting a simple design for a first project just so that you can finish it quickly and gain experience. Draw the design on a piece of paper approximately the same size as the wood surface. Move the design around on the wood until you find the best place-ment. Trace the letters onto the wood. For the sign illustrated, placing the letters diagonally across the square seemed most pleasing, and it gives the sign more balance. The letters are loosely based on an Old English style, only simplified and modified to suit a beginning project. Too elaborate a style can be frustrating, and the results may not be as clear.

The interior of the letters was regrooved with a small veiner, although any veiner or tool that suits you can be used. This design within the design makes the piece more decorative and also is good for cov-ering any slight imperfections that may occur when you carve the letters. Incised carving should not be done so perfectly that it appears as though a machine stamped out the letters. It is an imprecise art, and flaws are a part of the design and finished work. Each individual piece has its own unique characteristics.

Carving the Letters

After tracing the letters onto the wood, outline each letter with a very shallow running stop cut. The stop cuts will help prevent overrunning the boundaries of the letters and spoiling the crisp out-line. The stop cut should not be too deeply carved, and the triangular cut groove in the center of each

Fig. 5-37 *The paper design for the lettering is traced onto the wood with carbon paper.*

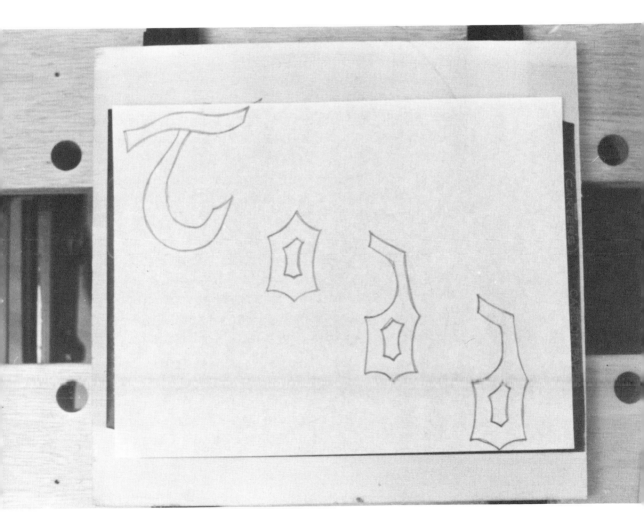

letter must be uniformly sloped down from the top surface. If the stop cuts are too deep, the letters will not be crisp, and they will seem to be off balance.

With a skew chisel, using minimal pressure, trace the outline boundaries (Fig. 5-38). Because pine is soft, it gives readily under a sharp blade.

After outlining the letters, start the groove down the center with a small veiner (Fig. 5-39). This cut need not be too deep; however, it should be deep enough that it does not become lost when the rest of the sides are carved away. When the letters are outlined and the center guide groove is cut, use a razor-sharp skew chisel to cut down either side of the letters. Cut slowly and with care in order to keep the slopes of the sides at the same angles. The sign will seem to be off balance if the angles vary too much.

If you are right-handed, grip the handle of the skew chisel with your right hand and place your left hand on the tool itself. The left hand will guide the tool while the right hand supplies the pressure.

The skew chisel and the veiner are adequate for this carving, but other tools will work just as well. Several tools were used in the pictures for demonstration purposes. The sheepfoot blade was used to do some outlining and then to carve out the groove in the center of the angles (Fig. 5-40). If you use this blade, grip the knife in your right hand and place your left hand closer to the blade edge. Keep in mind that with a shorter handle and a heavier blade on the knife, control is not as precise as with the skew chisel.

The one variable in this project is that you must work both with *and* against the grain. Depending on

Fig. 5-38 *Outlin-
ing the* **d** *with a
skew-tip chisel.*

Fig. 5-39 *Starting
the groove with a
small veiner.*

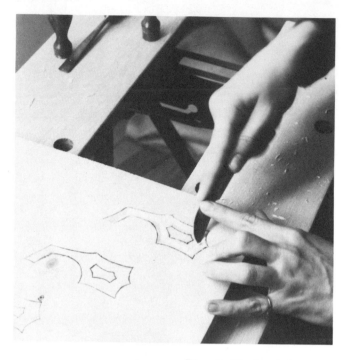

Fig. 5-40 *Incising the middle of the letter with a sheepfoot blade.*

the direction of the grain and the direction of the cut, you may have to vary the angle of the knife to prevent ripping and gouging the wood surface. Whenever possible, carving should be done *with* the grain (Fig. 5-41). Cutting across the grain can smash and crush the pores, and the finished appearance of the plaque will not be crisp and clear.

It may seem easier to do one side of the angle and then the other, but it is better to move evenly between the sides to keep the perspective accurate. Because evenness is the key to the finished appearance of each letter, strive for a balanced angle.

The center portion of each **d** should remain at the same level as the surrounding areas. Sanding will remove most of the dark trace lines, and the stain will cover the rest. It is more important to keep the top surface even than to worry about marks or mars that you can fix or cover later. Check the plaque from a distance from time to time to see if and where more wood needs to be removed and where it needs to be evened.

Carving the first letter is somewhat easier than the others because it will set the depth of the angled centers. The first letter in effect becomes the model. Use it to refer to the width of the angle, the depth, and the general configuration of the other letters (Figs. 5-42 and 5-43).

Figure 5-44 of the finished **d** shows how the top portion had to be angled (or placed) around the knot in the wood. Knots are circular patterns that are difficult to straight carve because they tend to chip or crush. Try to avoid knotty wood, unless you can make the knot an integral part of the design.

Fig. 5-41 *Angling the blade in order to cut with the grain.*

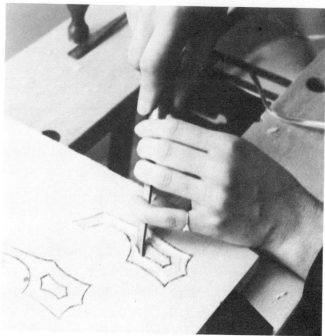

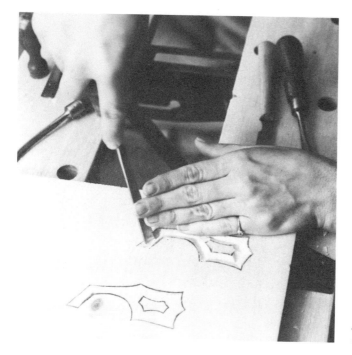

Fig. 5-42 *Using the $\frac{3}{8}''$ gouge to groove the middle of the letter.*

After completing the letter angles, use a small vein-er to make small grooves going straight downward to the base point. Overlap the grooves slightly to give the letter a finer texture. If you are making a larger sign with larger letters, the grooves obviously will be larger. Always experiment on scrap stock first before you commit yourself to a particular cut. Be careful that when you direct the veiner down the sides of the angle that you don't apply too much pressure; this may cause erratic grooves at the in-tersection of the angles, and it will keep the channel from being crisp. This newly carved surface should not be resistant to a sharp blade driven with minimal force. If it is, resharpen the blade before proceeding.

The **o** can be worked in much the same way as the **d**. The main concern with the **o** is the angled top section, which does not extend as the **d** does. This should have a clean point to distinguish it. It is not an elaborately decorative letter, but it should have a clean-lined simplicity.

The **T** has curved rather than angled lines. The top part of the letter dips and curves, and you must maintain the correct angle for consistent spacing. Because the **T** has a wider base angle, it should be more shallowly dished to keep the appearance more uniform with the narrower letters (Fig. 5-45). The angle sweeps to a sharp angled point like the other letters, but the entire span is shallowed and widened.

It is important with all the letters to stop cut the outline to prevent uneven boundaries. Stop-cutting the center of the **T** is even more important because of the wide curve. Without this kind of a guideline, it is hard to keep the perspective even. This letter is not "sectional" like the others, so your cuts must be clean.

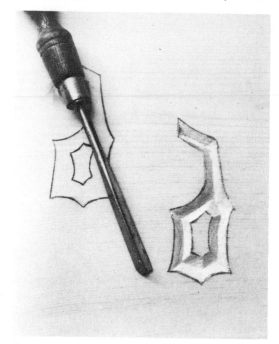

Fig. 5-43 *The evenly grooved* **d** *sets the depth for the other letters.*

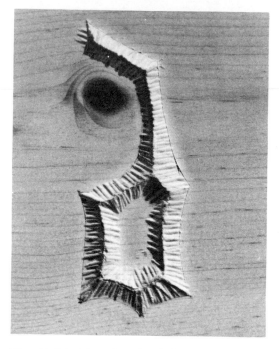

Fig. 5-44 *The finished letter, angled around a knot.*

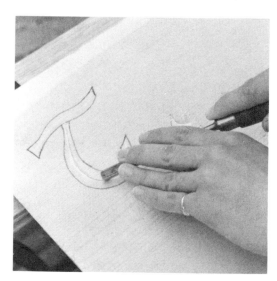

Fig. 5-45 *Using a veiner to carve the wider dished* **T.** *Each side of the curved portions is then beveled.*

Fig. 5-46 *The finished sign.*

After making the small grooves with the veiner, space them out a little bit over the curved portion. When you have made all the grooves, go back and fill in the gaps with small cuts that overlap the original cuts. All the veiner grooves should end at the center line. If they are not spaced and angled, they will start to slant sideways and ruin the balance of the curve.

Another suggestion is to start in the middle of the curve with the small veiner, then work outward from this center. Luckily, this type of texturing is forgiving of small errors and can be covered fairly easily, providing the errors are not too deep, too wide, or too glaring. Try each technique on scrap stock to see which you prefer. But remember that there are no specific "right" methods, only guidelines.

When you have textured all the letters, view the plaque from a distance to see if it appears to be complete as is, or if a decorative border would enhance it. A border was chosen for the "Todd" sign because the lettering is simple and unornamented. The border gives it an overall finished appearance. Because the lettering is simple and the pine grain nondistinct, a simple grooved border seemed appropriate. The grooves inside the letters and the border grooves compliment each other. The edge grooves were made with a U-tool, called a fluter. It has a tight curve at the base of the blade with almost straight sides. (This steepness of curve is referred to as a "quick curve".)

Almost any tool can be used to make a border. Many of the chip-carving triangular wedges would work well. Practice several cuts on scrap stock to determine which will compliment the style of your lettering. Be careful not to use too elaborate an edging that may clash with or overpower the design.

Working with the grain, drive the fluter toward the edge. Easy pressure is the key to keeping the grooves even. If the edging is uneven, it will look awkward and slanted.

After making the grooves, view the piece to see if they are adequate. If the letters have many overlapping tiny grooves, perhaps the pattern should be repeated as the edging. If so, cut additional grooves between the existing ones. The second grooving need not be as deep as the first if a rough-textured look is desired. Experiment first.

Sanding

Because pine is relatively smooth, the plaque needs only a light sanding with 220-grit sandpaper to remove any of the carbon paper marks and to open the grain for a good, even stain. Knots and other natural markings should be given particular attention. These will accept more stain and darken if you use a transparent finish. Sand lightly, and run your hand over the piece to locate any rough spots that may need more work. When the surface is smooth and blemish-free, begin the staining or sealing process.

Finishing

The sign in the illustrations was finished with brown wax shoe polish. This wax can cover several steps at once. The polish stains, seals, and polishes in only two steps. Smooth the wax by hand on the surface, taking care not to apply it too thickly. The rubbing must be done fairly evenly and without pausing too long before covering the entire front. If too much time lapses, the line between coats will become evident. Smooth from one side, then the other.

An alternative method of finishing is to apply clear polish to the letters and cover the rest of the surface with the darker wax. These letters were lightly touched with the brown to highlight the grooved texture of the interiors. Care was taken not to rub too much into them, which would then give them the same appearance as the raised area. Each coat of wax should be allowed to dry for about 30 minutes to an hour before buffing. Coating the piece effectively seals it from the elements.

The first coat of brown wax stains the pine a little darker than would a transparent wax. Most all woods darken somewhat regardless of the finish applied. The second coat gives the wood more of a cherry or walnut coloring and reveals more of the pine grain pattern. After the wax dries, buff it with a clean, soft cloth. An old terry-cloth towel does an excellent job if it does not shed lint.

The sides and back of the plaque were not sealed because the wood will not be exposed to drastic weather changes and conditions. But even an indoor sign plaque should be dusted periodically and, if necessary, recoated and buffed.

Relief Carving: Walnut Portrait Plaque

Portraitures, or picture plaques, are different from other types of carvings in that the end result must resemble the model as closely as possible. The first steps in portraiture are to make a series of drawings of the model, each with less detail until you have accurately achieved the least detail that delineates the prominent facial characteristics of the model. Unless you are carving an abstract face, the model should be recognizable.

For the plaque illustrated, which is $3\frac{1}{2}''$ by 5", the eye area and the mustache are the strongest features, so these areas needed the most delineation and refinement. However, if there is too much detail, the portrait will lose its simplistic texture, and the texture and grain of the wood will be lost as well. Instead, the wood should shine through and enhance the face.

Each line represents depth, not just detail. The lines should be carved at different widths and depths to define the facial structure. The deeper the lines, the heavier the feature or facial expression will appear. To become proficient at portraiture, you must first do a lot of experimenting with different knife blades and grips until you find those that suit the features and highlight the distinguishing characteristics of your model.

Selecting the Wood

Choose a piece of wood that is free of knots, burls, or other patterns. Any imperfections in the wood will detract from the facial features of the model. The color of the wood you choose is also important. For example, a fair-skinned, freckled person carved on a dark wood will appear as a photographic negative. A fair-skinned person will reproduce much better on a clear pine or maple plaque. On the other hand, a person with a darker complexion would look odd and too delicate on a light wood like pine. Choose the wood to compliment the coloring and the features of your model. This is not a hard and fast rule, but with a first portrait especially, try to forego experimentation until you have made several realistic portraits.

Making the Drawing

If you want to highlight the wood rather than the model's face, you could make an old-fashioned silhouette. To make the drawing, have the model sit in profile against a wall in front of a strong light. On drawing paper, trace the outline of the shadow that is cast on the wall. Then reduce the drawing and transfer it to the wood. Silhouettes are particularly good for children's faces because any heavy carved detail will tend to add age to their delicate features. Keeping carved detail to a minimum allows the wood to be the focal point.

Another method in portraiture is to use photographs, one front view and one profile. Checking back and forth between the two pictures will allow you to keep the features in proportion and also make the resemblance easier to capture. Then transfer the likeness to the wood. You may center the likeness by eye, and then shape the edges with a router (Fig. 5-47). To frame the face within the routed edging, use a small U-tool to cut a narrow path around the inside of the smooth top surface (Fig. 5-48).

Carving The Blank

Before carving the features, make stop cuts around all the lines of the face with a straight razor or sharp, pointed knife blade. These cuts will help prevent the blade from slipping and cutting too far over the line and help prevent gouging the wood and ripping it. Hold the knife in the jeweler's grip and carefully push into the wood (Fig. 5-49). Do not attempt to cut too deeply or in too long a length at a time. Otherwise, the blade can slip and cause the gouges that the stop cuts are made to prevent.

After making the stop cuts, start carefully with one of the wider features, such as the laugh lines around the nose and mouth (Fig. 5-50). Wedge-cut small amounts at a time. The face illustrated had

Fig. 5-47 *The drawing of the model centered and sketched on the plaque.*

Fig. 5-48 *Outlining the border with a small U-tool.*

fairly deep lines, so the initial cut was deep but then curved gradually to form the cheek area.

A substantial amount of wood must be removed from the eye area. Eyebrows are usually heavier than the nose and mouth area, especially in men. Children and women are generally much lighter and more rounded. Use the model as the guide.

To help balance the entire plaque and give some idea of the appropriate depth around the face, use a $\frac{1}{16}$" U-tool to remove some of the background (Fig. 5-51). Carve slowly and evenly to prevent gouging the base too deeply. It helps to hold the tool with your finger on top guiding and regulating the pressure.

The area under the chin can be difficult. Decide whether or not you will include the neck as part of the portrait and how much depth you will need in contrast to the chin. The chin area of this model is full, so a slight emphasis was placed on the neck. There are three levels to the plaque: (1) the background, (2) the neck area, and (3) the face itself. The levels vary only slightly. Too great a definition between the face and neck would detract from the model's features. If you are making an abstract portrait that is not intended to resemble anyone in particular, it is not as crucial to follow a model precisely. Abstracts permit greater freedom for individual expression.

After determining the background depth, take the smaller U-tool and outline around the profile (Fig. 5-52). This tool will help prevent removing too much wood. When carving along this crucial area, don't carve too close to the actual drawn line, or you will risk removing part of the profile features. Start about $\frac{1}{4}$ inch away from the line and work slowly in. Be

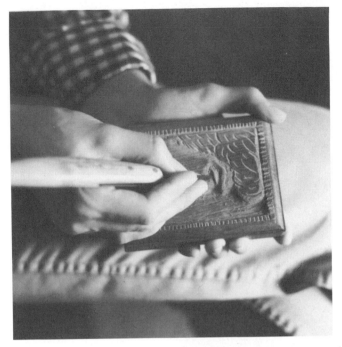

Fig. 5-49 *Making stop cuts around the facial lines with a skew-tip.*

Fig. 5-50 *Small wedge cuts made with a spear-tip blade help to define the more prominent features.*

Fig. 5-51 *Defining the depth of relief around the face with a U-tool.*

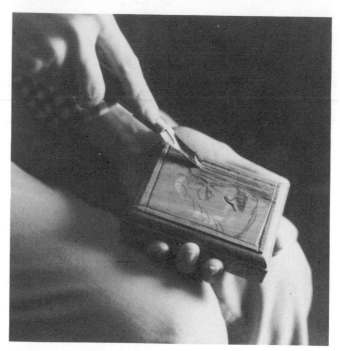

Fig. 5-52 *Using the U-tool to outline the profile.*

Fig. 5-53 *Adding finishing touches to the border of the plaque with the U-tool.*

Fig. 5-54 *Smoothing the rough-cut features with a sheepfoot.*

patient on this part. Whereas other types of carvings can be blended and "fixed," when a portrait is of a specific person, there is little altering that can be done without altering the appearance of the model.

Study the model and the piece to determine where changes need to be made. Sometimes only very subtle touches need to be made to make the face come alive. Look for such seemingly small details as the nostril flare, the tilt of the eye sockets, or the corners of the mouth.

About midpoint in the process of carving the plaque illustrated here, something seemed to be missing and an unplanned step was added. The outside edge did not look like a frame. Because the picture is small, the edging needed something more to dress it up. Small perpendicular cuts were made around the edge (Fig. 5-53). They were simply carved out with the same small U-tool used to do the profile.

The hair can be lightly textured by removing only a few curved areas to simulate thick wavy hair. Try out any ideas first on scrap wood of the same stock. Holding the knife in the jeweler's grip should allow you to produce most any type of hair texture, but experiment with different blades and techniques.

After carving the features in the rough, go over them with a sharp sheepfoot blade and refine any rough areas. Use a sheepfoot blade to smooth and define the jaw and chin lines. The tip of the sheepfoot was used here to texture the heavy mustache (Fig. 5-54). It was wedged at spaced intervals to give the appearance of thickness to the upper lip and mustache.

A finer-tipped, elongated sheepfoot blade held in the jeweler's grip was used to cut the area around the eyeball. The socket, like the neck area, had to

Fig. 5-55 *The sheepfoot can also be used to texture the prominent features such as the mustache, eyebrows, eye socket, and nostrils.*

Fig. 5-56 *Shaving uneven carving marks with a small, angled skew-tip chisel.*

be delineated from the surrounding area (Fig. 5-55). The brow lines and the nostrils were defined and refined with the same blade and grip.

Such longer, smoother lines as the nose and cheeks were smoothed with a small, angled skew-tip chisel (Fig. 5-56). The blade must be very sharp to shave off the rougher wood "hairs" that come from uneven carving. When a piece is as small as the one illustrated, some mars are inevitable.

This shaving method removes them easily, although be careful not to gouge the wood.

Finishing

Smooth any rough spots before finishing the plaque. Finishing a plaque requires a great deal of time, patience, *and* sandpaper. Sandpaper can remove some of the more subtle nuances of the face. Start with a fine sandpaper, such as 150-grit aluminum oxide. This grit is rough enough to smooth the tool marks yet is gentle enough to leave the features intact. After sanding, wet the wood to raise the grain and allow it to dry. Then sand lightly with 220-grit paper in the direction of the grain. This plaque was buffed with a light oil and then waxed to a fine sheen.

Abstract Forms

Abstract art can be defined as the opposite of representational art. If representational carvings are realistic imitations of nature, then abstracts are anything *else*. An abstract woodcarving or sculpture is more easily defined by what it is not, rather than by what it is. And rarely does it have only one interpretation. It does not follow the conventional and traditional rules and concepts of carving from nature, but rather is unique and individual, having its own identity.

Fig. 5-57 *"Safety Net," by John Reida. A dramatic piece that can be interpreted in several ways: the hands may appear to be climbing upward, or slipping away, losing their grasp. And what are they climbing to, or slipping from? Whatever the eye and the imagination can conjure. Reida says much with this piece, yet says it very subtly.*

Fig. 5-58 *Untitled freeform, by John Reida. The dark, smooth walnut suggests graceful and even motion. Smoothly carved-out spaces give the piece a light, airy appearance, where the mass of dark wood might otherwise have appeared to be weighed down.*

The one word that is descriptive of abstract pieces is *intrinsic*. The feel, idea, and mood come from *inside* the artist. An abstract sculpture may or may not be aesthetically pleasing or appealing to an audience, but it is never "wrong." Any expression of the artist, if it is honest, is valid. For this very reason, there is no step-by-step guide for this chapter. Once you have mastered the tools and carving techniques and learn about the various types of wood, you can experiment with your own abstract forms. Use examples of the works of other artists as a stepping-off point.

Abstract woodcarving is often difficult for the beginner because of the number of elements that must be considered in the design and execution. The "theory" of carving abstracts has changed dramatically in the past several years. No longer must strict rules of design be incorporated to give a piece credibility.

Fig. 5-59 "Beggar Woman," by John Reida. The posture and dark, recessed face indicate a forlorn figure. The thinness of the carved line at the upper torso suggests a fragile shawl, clutched tightly about the body, with the roughly textured finish completing the image.

Fig. 5-60 "Waiting," by John Reida. The figure, in solid heavy walnut, broods while it waits patiently. The straight vertical grain adds to the stationary feel; the pose does not even suggest motion. The head is held high, the body erect, with a quiet dignity, reminiscent of a serene, solitary church figurine.

Fig. 5-61 *Untitled sculpture by John Reida. This work suggests a nunlike figure, approaching the viewer. The wood was split at a quarter-angle and seasoned in this shape to show off the grain and to lend motion to the carved figure. The vertical grain lines come together in front of the figure, causing the eye to travel along these lines, creating an illusion of motion.*

Any combination or even the rejection of some or all of the former principles allows the artist freedom to carve and interpret individually.

Basic elements such as balance, shape, motion, proportion, and dimension should be considered in your first designs. Sketches are more important for abstracts because of the absolute freedom during carving to mold and shape the wood. It becomes too easy to keep removing the wood and end with a miniature nothing. The basic sketches help you keep the proportion, mood, and dimensions in mind throughout the carving process. This is not to say that you cannot or should not change the balance or symmetry during the carving process if new inspiration strikes. This is just one more guideline, and it applies to the beginner and master alike.

Representational forms and figures are absolute. A representational carving of a squirrel, for example, is a squirrel. The more abstract the squirrel becomes, the more open it is to another interpretation. Details are one of the major differences between the real and the abstract. The more detail that is added to a realistic piece defines and sharpens the shape, whereas the more detail added to an abstract piece may have nothing to do with shape.

Following the basic elements of design will allow you to see the endless possibilities and innovations in wood carving. Keeping in mind these basics should open new doors as you become experienced. Abstraction is simply one more style in woodcarving that you can experiment with while exploring your artistic potential.

CHAPTER 6

Clark Mester: Portrait of a Wood Sculptor

CLARK MESTER is an accomplished professional artist and sculptor who had no formal art training until after he finished college. With a degree in Business, he taught high school and coached athletics for several years; eventually deciding to become a full-time art student at Morgan State in Baltimore. He soon immersed himself full-time in art education.

Clark's encouragement and inspiration came from two of his teachers at Morgan, James E. Lewis and Dr. Randall Craig, both outstanding innovators in figurative sculpture.

"Nothing is obvious. Take nothing for granted," is Clark's advice to beginning woodcarvers. He feels that his best expression is revealed in wood. The material is the motivation: "The wood talks to me. It lives and breathes. The smell, texture, feel are very real." The strength of Clark's sculptures are a direct reflection of his physical stature, yet the gentleness of the lines bespeak an underlying sensitivity for the wood and the design. Each piece is done only once, and each is a complete statement or, as in his *Life Series*, one idea flows into another and is either in-

Fig. 6-1 Life Series I.

Fig. 6-2 Life Series III.

terpreted individually or as a cycle or progression of concepts. There is humor in the pieces as well as an understanding of the intricacies of body language.

Clark draws or makes his model first to determine proportion and line. Then he selects the wood. Sometimes the wood dictates what the form will be. Knots, burls, unique grain configurations, color, and texture are all considerations that help him draft the finished piece. He often works with large logs, sometimes five feet or longer, so his small maquettes become important references for his work.

With the log on the floor of his studio work area, Clark methodically and laboriously begins the work of debarking. He uses an adz to remove the tough outer layer of the bark, almost straddling the log and striking in a downward motion toward his feet. Clark's proficiency with the tool and years of practice allow him to work this way. The novice, however, should always strike away from the body to prevent injury.

After most of the bark is removed, Clark places the log on sawhorses and continues the heavy work with a wide chisel and large mallet. When the log is free of bark, he roughs out the form and waxes the entire piece to prevent moisture loss and the inevitable cracking and checking. Parts that do check are filled with wax and later blended with the finish.

With the waxed log on the sawhorses, Clark begins the actual carving, usually with a moderate weight mallet and large chisel. He carefully cuts in a circular motion around the knots that he uncovers. Working around the piece, he turns it to reach all sides. There is an ease in his carving that comes from an intimate knowledge of his tools and the wood. Nothing is left to chance. Every strike is deliberate. Occasionally

Fig. 6-3 *The artist at work.*

Fig. 6-4 *Debarking a log with an adz.*

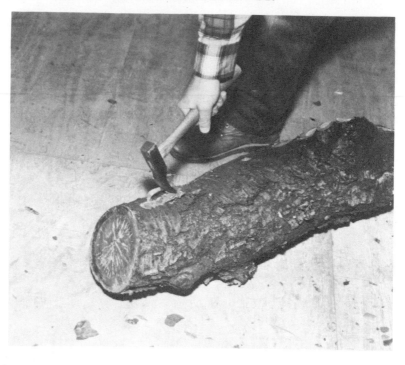

Fig. 6-5 *Continuing the debarking with a large chisel and mallet. The log is placed on sawhorses.*

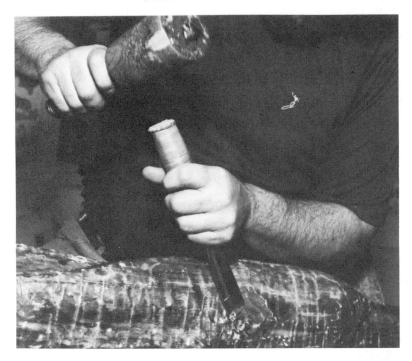

Fig. 6-6 *Carving in a circular motion around a knot.*

Fig. 6-7 *Carving to smooth the area around the knot is done with the grain.*

he pauses to make pencil marks or lines on the piece to help guide him to the proportion he wants.

After the work is completed, Clark sands and smoothes the piece and applies the finish. He chooses his base for the sculpture as carefully as he chooses the wood and design. In *Life Series III* (Fig. 6-2), the design contrasts with the "bed" of flat, straight-lined oak. The piece itself is cedar, oak, and walnut. The oak is reflected in the base and contrasts with the dark walnut.

The method Clark uses to design a sculpture is an excellent one for the beginning artist and carver. On a blank sheet of drawing paper, he freely makes abstract swirls and waves that overlap and converge until they cover the page. Then he views the entire

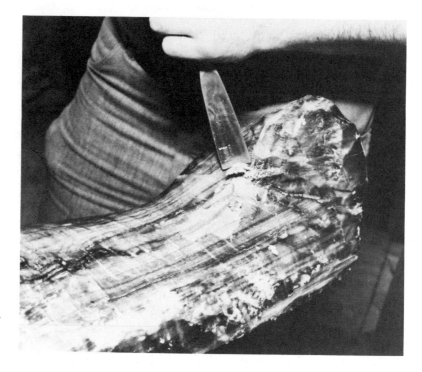

Fig. 6-8 *Clark Mester often incorporates sapwood in his designs. Because it is so soft, the sapwood must be worked carefully.*

Fig. 6-9 *The slow, magical transformation of a felled log into a sculpture. This seven-foot piece, unfinished and yet to be titled, is still coated with wax.*

abstract with an eye for shape and pattern. There may be one shape or many shapes that catch his eye in any one drawing. Clark uses his senses to "feel" the balance and proportion of the final design. Many of his pieces come directly from his imagination onto the page or into a wax maquette. Some of his maquettes he later casts in bronze, and they populate his studio as though it were a miniature gallery in itself.

Clark works in a huge studio in Baltimore that he shares with a sculptor and ceramist. He describes his time in the studio as his "refuge and island" in a rather full life. Along with teaching, sculpting, and bronze casting, Clark frequently shows his work and conducts workshops nationally.

The studio—a large working space, an open area for display, and a smaller area for relaxing and designing—reflects an artist who not only lives his work, but who enjoys it to the fullest.

Glossary

Annual Ring—The layer of wood formed around the tree stem in one growing season. Also called a ting.

Bas-Relief—A two-dimensional carving, where the background is recessed from the carved relief. Many bas-reliefs fall just short of being in-the-round.

Bevel—The sloping angle on the blade edge, or the sloped edge of wood in incised carving.

Bosting—The first rough cutting of a wood blank to shape the outlines of the design.

Check—A crack or split that occurs naturally in the wood, usually on the rays, or from improper seasoning and handling.

Chip Carving—Forming a design by removing wedge-shaped pieces of wood. These triangular cuts can be arranged geometrically to form a border on a plaque, or they can form a specific design in themselves.

Chisel—A bevel-edged tool with a straight blade. It is driven with either hand pressure or mallet force.

Clamp—A wooden or metal tool used to stabilize a piece of wood for carving.

Cross-cut—Cutting across the grain.

Dished—Making a cut from an angle to slope the sides.

End Grain—The pattern of the fibers exposed after cross-cutting a piece of stock. Literally, the end of the grain.

Face Grain—The grain pattern exposed when a log or piece of wood is cut lengthwise.

Figure—The design or distinguishable pattern evident on a piece of stock. These markings distinguish one type of wood from another.

File—An abrasive tool used to smooth or remove wood from the surface of a piece. Files are available in a wide variety of sizes and grades of roughness, which determines the quantity of wood removed.

Finishing—The final stage in woodcarving that smoothes or colors the wood surface and coats it for lasting protection and maximum appearance.

Fluter—A small gouge with tight (quick) curves.

Gouges—Woodcarving tools with curved blades, rather than straight like chisels. An immense variety of curves and sizes are widely available.

Grain—The structure of the wood pattern that is evident when the wood is cut crosswise or lengthwise. The pores, resin canals, and the density of the wood comprise the grain pattern.

Green Wood—Wood before it has been seasoned and dried to prevent checks or warping. It has nothing to do with the color of the wood.

Hardwood—Technically, the wood from a deciduous tree. However, in woodcarving it is more a reference of the hardness of the wood to the tool and the touch.

Heartwood—The hard inner portion of the tree that is the best wood for carving. The heartwood is characterized by its hardness and generally dark color.

Incised Carving—Cutting incisions in grooved patterns into the wood. It is a two-dimensional carving.

In-the-Round—Three-dimensional carving or whittling.

Low Relief—A type of carving where the background is in-cised, leaving the foreground as the picture or design. The depth is shallow, the relief not very high.

Mallet—A hardwood tool (generally made of imported, *extremely* hard woods) used to force a chisel or gouge into wood. The mallet is held several inches from the tool handle and is either tapped or forcefully driven.

Rasp—A metal file with large, coarse teeth and, thus, more abrading ability than a regular file.

Sapwood—The softer, light-colored young wood that con-tains the living cells that transport the sap throughout the trunk and limbs. As the tree matures, sapwood be-comes heartwood.

Seasoning—Removing the moisture from wood to prevent checks and cracks. Wood can be seasoned by air- or kiln-drying, or it can be soaked in polyethelene glycoe.

Slip—An oilstone that is used to sharpen the curve of a gouge or V-tool.

Soft wood—Technically, the wood from a coniferous tree. However, in woodcarving, it is used to denote the ease of carving.

Stock—The piece of wood ready to be carved or whittled.

Stop Cut—A cut made in the wood to protect against cutting too far over the outline. Outlining cuts are often stop cuts. These cuts are made vertically into the surface.

V-Tool—A double-sided chisel shaped like a V, used to cut grooves.

Veiner—A small, "quick" (sharply angled) gouge.

Warping—The action of improperly dried wood, which twists and bends out of shape while being worked.

Whittling—Three-dimensional carving. Usually the piece is small enough to be held in the hand while being carved.

List of Suppliers

Woods and Woodcarving Tools

Craftsman Wood Service
    2727 South Mary Street
    Chicago, IL 60608

M & M Hardwood
    53344 Vineland Avenue
    North Hollywood, CA
    91601

Sculpture Associates
    114 East 25th Street
    New York, NY 10010

Sculpture Services, Inc.
    9 East 19th Street
    New York, NY 10003

Finishing Products

H. Behlen and Brothers, Inc.
    P. O. Box 698
    Amsterdam, NY 12010

Minwax Company, Inc.
    72 Oak Street
    Clifton, NJ 07014

Woodcraft Supply Corporation
    313 Montvale Avenue
    Woburn, MA 01801

Index

Page numbers in **bold** refer to illustrations.